"In this book, John Michael Talbot returns to the roots of Christian monasticism and, based on his own lived experience, comments on the Rule of Benedict, not as a contribution to scientific research, but to make the spiritual riches of this Rule fruitful for us contemporary men and women. He reads the Rule with a modern eye and opens it up as much for people who live in a community as those living in the world of everyday work. For this reason, these meditations are also suitable for Benedictine secular oblates. A life based on the principles of the Rule of Benedict makes the world a more Christian and more human place. And with this, Benedict himself becomes a blessing for our times."

—Notker Wolf, OSB
Abbot Primate of the Benedictine Order

# Blessings of St. Benedict

John Michael Talbot

LITURGICAL PRESS
Collegeville, Minnesota

www.litpress.org

Cover design by David Manahan, OSB. Illustration and fresco of St. Benedict at Sacro Speco, Subiaco.

© 2011 by Order of Saint Benedict, Collegeville, Minnesota. All rights reserved. No part of this book may be reproduced in any form, by print, microfilm, microfiche, mechanical recording, photocopying, translation, or by any other means, known or yet unknown, for any purpose except brief quotations in reviews, without the previous written permission of Liturgical Press, Saint John's Abbey, PO Box 7500, Collegeville, Minnesota 56321-7500. Printed in the United States of America.

| 1 | 2 | 3 | 4 | 5 | 6 | 7 | 8 |
|---|---|---|---|---|---|---|---|

**Library of Congress Cataloging-in-Publication Data**

Talbot, John Michael.
  Blessings of St. Benedict / John Michael Talbot.
      p.    cm.
  ISBN 978-0-8146-3385-4 (pbk.) — ISBN 978-0-8146-3386-1 (e-book)
    1. Benedict, Saint, Abbot of Monte Cassino. Regula.
  2. Meditations.   I. Title.   II. Title: Blessings of Saint Benedict.

BX3004.Z5T35   2011

255'.106—dc23                                                            2011021156

*In memory of*
*Abbot Timothy Kelly, OSB*
*Friend and Teacher*
*1934–2010*

# Contents

Introduction: The Blessings of St. Benedict   1

Prologue: Listen   5

Prologue: Letting Go of Self-Will   7

Prologue: A School of the Lord's Service   9

Chapter 1: Kinds of Monks   11

Chapter 2: The Qualities of the Abbot   14

Chapter 3: Calling the Brothers and Sisters for Counsel   16

Chapter 4: The Tools for Good Works   18

Chapter 5: Obedience   20

Chapter 6: Silence and Restraint of Speech   22

Chapter 7: Humility   24

Chapters 8–20: The Work of God, the Divine Office   27

Chapter 13: Time and Character of the Offices   30

Chapter 21: The Deans of the Monastery   32

Chapter 22: The Sleeping Arrangements of the Monks   34

Chapter 23–28: Monastic Excommunication   36

Chapter 29: Readmission of Brothers Who Leave the Monastery   39

Chapter 30: Children and the Manner of Reproving Boys   41

Chapter 31: The Cellarer   43

Chapter 32: The Tools and Goods of the Monastery   45

Chapter 33: Private Ownership and Monks   47

Chapter 34: Distribution of Goods   49

Chapter 35: Kitchen Servers of the Week   51

Chapter 36: The Sick Brothers   53

Chapter 37: The Elderly and Children   55

Chapter 38: The Weekly Readers   57

Chapter 39: The Proper Amount of Food   59

Chapter 40: The Proper Amount of Drink   61

Chapter 41: The Times for Meals   63

Chapter 42: Silence after Compline   65

Chapter 43: Tardiness   67

Chapter 44: Satisfaction and Forgiveness   69

Chapter 45: Mistakes in Church   71

Chapter 46: Faults in Other Matters   73

Chapter 47: Announcing the Work of God   75

Chapter 48: Manual Labor and Reading   77

Chapter 49: The Observance of Lent   79

Chapters 50–51: Monks Working at a Distance
or Traveling and on a Short Journey    81

Chapter 52: The Oratory of the Monastery    83

Chapter 53: The Reception of Guests    85

Chapter 54: Letters and Gifts for Monks    87

Chapter 55: The Clothing, Footwear, and Bedding
of the Monks    89

Chapter 56: The Abbot's Table    91

Chapter 57: The Artisans of the Monastery    93

Chapter 58: The Procedure for Receiving
New Brothers    95

Chapter 59: The Offering of Sons by Nobles
or by the Poor    98

Chapter 60: The Admission of Priests
to the Monastery    100

Chapter 61: The Reception of Visiting Monks    103

Chapter 62: The Priests of the Monastery    106

Chapter 63: Community Rank    108

Chapter 64: The Election of the Abbot    110

Chapter 65: The Prior    112

Chapter 66: The Porter of the Monastery    114

Chapter 67: Brothers Sent on a Journey    116

Chapter 68: The Assignment of Impossible Tasks
to a Brother    118

Chapter 69: The Presumption of Defending Another
in the Monastery    120

Chapter 70: The Presumption of Striking Another
  Monk at Will   122

Chapter 71: Mutual Obedience   124

Chapter 72: The Good Zeal of Monks   126

Chapter 73: The Rule: Only a Beginning
  of Perfection   128

Introduction

# The Blessings of St. Benedict

This little book is a collection of blessings from St. Benedict. "Benedict" has the same root as "benediction" or "blessing." Little is known of this great Western saint. Besides his Rule and the Life by St. Gregory the Great, there is nothing originally written about him. But his effect on the world is profound.

His Rule guided communities that brought forth saints that shaped the Western world and beyond. The Benedictines Augustine of Canterbury evangelized Britain, and Boniface, Germany. The Celts used Benedict's rule of life as they spread through continental Europe. The great house of and spiritual movement from Cluny shaped religious life and spread Christianity throughout Europe in the ninth and tenth centuries. St. Bernard of Clairvaux, called the greatest man in Europe in his day, was a powerhouse of the Cistercian Benedictine reform of the eleventh century. St. Peter Damien was another great preacher and churchman of that century who represents the Benedictine hermit tradition from the Camaldolese of St. Romuald. The Benedictines made huge scientific and theological advances with things as basic as the creation of the modern plough for agriculture, and they maintained European

## 2 Blessings of St. Benedict

civilization during the Black Death. More recently, the reform at Solesmes in France brought a revival of Gregorian chant that has blessed the world through, for example, the best-selling recordings at Santa Domingo in Spain. The Benedictines helped pioneer America and set up centers of education based on contemplation, study, and community life that have brought forth thousands of graduates who have had a profound effect on the well-being of our nation. These are just some of the effects the Rule of St. Benedict has had not only on the Catholic Church but also on civilization as we know it.

The Rule calls itself "a little rule for beginners," but it is built on a monastic tradition that predates it by hundreds of years. The *Conferences* and *Institutes* of John Cassian, St. Basil's Rules, and the teaching and Lives of the Fathers are mentioned in it as sources for the more advanced. But such self-deprecations were not to be long-lived. The Rule masterfully harmonizes the past great traditions of monasticism and liturgy. The Rule has served as a basis for a way of life because it simply works. It is highly challenging but imminently practical. That is why it spread almost universally in the Christian West among most monastic communities before the rise of the canons and mendicants in the eleventh and thirteenth centuries.

The Rule comes from a time long ago. Parts of it are timeless, and other parts are reflective of sixteen hundred years ago when Benedict wrote the Rule. Initially some of it is culturally off-putting to the modern reader, but even these chapters have something to teach those who are willing to look patiently beneath the text to the timeless.

We use the Rule in our integrated monastery at Little Portion Hermitage and Monastery. While birthed from the Franciscan tradition, we have found that the Rule of St. Benedict is the best inspiration for the day in and day out life of the monastery. We read it, as well as commentaries on it, often at meals. I teach it in community meetings once a year or so.

These little meditations are based on more in-depth study but are meant to be simple and uplifting. They are for monks and those who are simply monks at heart and live in the secular world. They are supposed to be read to aid in prayer and meditation. I hope it helps with both.

I hope you enjoy this little book as much as I have enjoyed writing it. I hope it brings Jesus more deeply into your daily life. I pray that it is a blessing for you that comes not from me but from St. Benedict.

## Prologue

# Listen

*"Listen carefully, my son, to a master's instructions . . . from a father who loves you"* (Prol 1).

The Prologue of the Rule of St. Benedict begins with an admonition to listen to a father who loves his spiritual child. All the rest follows from this. In order to listen we must first be silent. We cannot listen if we are constantly talking, or objecting, or forming our answers. We cannot listen if our thoughts, emotions, or bodily senses are always crying out noisily. We must be still and listen.

A good discipline for me is to let a person finish speaking before I start. I try to hear them before I formulate my response. I try to get beyond their ability to speak well, or even to speak the lingo, or in the way I like. I try to hear their heart, their soul, and their spirit. I try to hear their person and not just their personality. That is the deeper reality.

In order to do this I must first be still and get in touch with my own deepest spirit, soul, and heart. I must pray before I talk and sit still in meditation before I act. I still my body through my posture and breath, then my thoughts and emotions settle down. Then my own spirit emerges so I can really hear the other person spirit to spirit, soul to soul, and heart to heart.

Listening to others is just the beginning. We must also listen to God. Listening to religious leaders is just practice for listening to God. It gives us an incarnational environment to flesh out if we can really listen at all. Otherwise our prayers, meditations, and theological studies might just be an illusion. It is good to flesh out our listening with a trusted leader.

Listening to superiors is also practice for listening to everyone and everything in meditative stillness. Only when we learn to listen can we know what to say when we speak.

We listen to a father or mother who loves us. They are not there to control or manipulate us. They are older and trusted ones who guide us on our spiritual journey as a gift of love. They are there to help set us free, not to bind us. Good and trusted leaders are a great gift from God. We do well to listen to them.

Listening to a leader and brothers and sisters is a conduit for the voice of God. Even the pope must listen to the sense of the faithful before he can speak formally *ex cathedra*, or with the assurance of the infallibility of the Holy Spirit as promised by Jesus Christ.

Are we listening today? Be still. Breathe. Listen. Then we will know what we are to say, and what we say will be a blessing to this world.

## Prologue

# Letting Go of Self-Will

*"If you are ready to give up your own will, once and for all . . . " (Prol 3).*

Letting go of self-will is a theme that echoes through the Rule of St. Benedict. It may sound restrictive at first, but it is one of the most liberating things about it in the long run. It can sound like a curse to some, but it is a great blessing to all who accept it fully.

The human will is part of who we are. It is a gift from God. It is distinct from mere emotions or cold thought but includes them both in the heart of love. If anything, we need people who live by the will to love and not by brute emotions or cold and calculating thoughts alone.

It is not that the human will is bad, but we have often used it badly. The will is the faculty of decision. Love is a decision, so the will is the seat of love. Love is self-emptying for the sake of another that produces new life in others and in ourselves.

Jesus says we must renounce our self to follow him. St. Paul says we die to the old self in baptism so that we can rise up a new person in Jesus. That old self is the person who used the will badly. Bad choices hurt others as well as ourselves.

The old self is the person we allowed ourselves to become, not the person God made us to be. The old self does not make us happy and does not make others happy. We must renounce it in order to regain who we really are in God and be happy.

Scripture says that we are spirit, soul, and body (1 Thess 5:23). We are a united harmony of all three. The spirit is the essence of who we are and exists in a wonderful world that goes beyond space or time, beyond senses, emotions, or thoughts. The soul and body are the human energies. The essence enlivens the energies, which in turn give form to essence. The soul is the spiritual mind that processes the things of space and time. The body uses the senses that house this spiritual wonder in God's creation. The problem is that we have gotten turned upside down and now see ourselves from a predominantly sensual, emotional, and mental perspective. The spiritual gets relegated to a nice belief but something that rarely inspires our daily life. It is an incomplete existence. Through his cross, Jesus turns us right side up when we die to the old self of upside-down priorities so that we can rise through his resurrection and be fully alive in him again!

The Rule calls us to give up self-will "once and for all." If we keep toying with its temptations or possibilities then we are never really free. As Jesus says, "The good plowman does not look back." We must have done with it once and for all! Only when we let go of ourselves do we find out who we are in Christ. We rediscover who God made us to be. This is a blessing beyond earthly value but blesses our entire life on earth and in heaven. It is a blessing of St. Benedict.

Prologue

# A School of the Lord's Service

*"Therefore we intend to establish a school for the Lord's service" (Prol 45).*

Life is a school. The church is a school where we learn how to follow Jesus, the author and giver of life. We must learn how to live if we are to live well. It does not always come automatically. Jesus is our greatest teacher.

The monastery is the schoolhouse where we learn how to be better disciples of Jesus. Like all schools, there are some rules and disciplines we embrace, but a place of real learning is not just about hard work and study. There is joy in learning. That joy in learning far outweighs the hard work of study and enriches our life.

The leaders of the community stand in the place of Jesus on earth. They try to live like Jesus and lead us to Jesus. Most of the time they do pretty well, but sometimes they fail, just as we all do. To see this wonder of Christ's presence through them we must look with the eyes of faith. Otherwise we will only see their failings and faults.

Each of us has our own monastery within. When we realize this, each family, workplace, or parish becomes a school of the Lord's service. We discover with St. Francis that "the world is my cloister, my body is my cell, and my soul is the hermit within." We take the monastery everywhere we go.

Nothing too harsh is established here. Most rules and disciplines are just about working together in harmony and leading each other to Jesus. But even a spiritual school must deal with food, clothing, and shelter, plus making a living. Life on earth requires work in the world of physical, emotional, and intellectual phenomenon. But the sacrifices we make for the greater good of the community enrich our individual lives as well.

In this school of God we live in community with others. Life with others causes us to examine ourselves. We love others, as we would like to be loved ourselves. This isn't always easy. We were not born into this monastic family. Jesus chose us and we responded. But others responded too. We must follow Jesus with them or we cannot really follow him at all. We might think we love Jesus, but sometimes we don't like others that much. There's the rub. We must learn how to love others as well. After some time we may even discover that we actually like them. Eventually some even become our close spiritual friends.

The text of the Rule says not to run quickly away when we face something difficult in the way of life described by the Rule. Sometimes when we face something difficult we want to run away. The Rule encourages us not to. If we do, we often rob ourselves of the greater blessing. Plus, we are usually bound to just repeat it again somewhere else if we do not deal with it now. Many of things we dislike most in our outer environment stem from things we dislike within ourselves. These must be courageously faced and brought to the forgiveness of Jesus. Then we can be set free, once and for all. Then we can be blessed. This is a great blessing of monastic community as described by Benedict.

## Chapter 1

# Kinds of Monks

The monk is one who lives for God and God alone. In so doing, the monk becomes a blessing to everyone and everything he or she meets. The monk is "separated from all, and united with all" (Evagrius Ponticus). The monk is a blessing, even as St. Benedict was a blessing.

There were all kinds of monks in the early church. They ranged from informal groups in family houses to formal communities in or on the outskirts of towns to those who dwelt in deserted places alone or together. Some stayed in one place, and some used their monasteries as bases of ministry. They existed from one end of the Christian world to the other, though Egypt came to be seen as the archetypical monastic example. There was no one pattern, though some were seen as superior to others.

The Rule mentions four kinds of people who follow Jesus in monastic life: Those who live alone as hermits, those who live in community as cenobites, those who follow their own will and call it monasticism as sarabaites, and those who wander aimlessly from monastery to monastery as gyrovagues. While these names are old, we see our own versions of them today under different names and forms.

It is hard to live alone, and it is hard to live with others. It is hard to give up our own will, and it is hard to settle down. We all face something of each kind of monk within ourselves.

We also see it in society. Some cannot get along with others so they close themselves off in isolation. Some cannot stand to be alone so they occupy their lives in a constant stream of social activity. Some cannot let go of their own wills so they are never happy with themselves. And some cannot settle down with one thing or person so they end up wandering all their lives from place to place.

Those who want to live alone must not try to escape the love responsibility of relationships with others in family and community. Those who want community must not run from solitude. Community must flow from the face-to-face encounter with Jesus found in solitude, and solitude must overflow into love relationships in Christ. Solitude flows into community, and community leads back into solitude. We find Jesus in both places.

We must also renounce our old self-will if we are to be born again in Christ and discover who we are in God. Once we do this, we may travel far in life but we will always be at home. We will bring stability to a world where even the basic fabric of civilization and human being itself is breaking apart. We will be a blessing from God for everyone we meet.

Monks make commitments to God and others based on love, and they keep those commitments. They do not abandon their loved ones and shirk their responsibilities. The strength of our faith isn't tested when all is going well but when it is most difficult. The spiritual chain of our faith is only as strong as its weakest link. All of us are called to be faithful to spouses and families as well as to church and faith communities so that we may strengthen this world that is in such peril of collapse. This is a great blessing offered by Benedict to the world today, especially in the West. The Rule offers genuine solitude and community, stability and freedom. It is a blessing of St. Benedict.

## Chapter 2

# The Qualities of the Abbot

We are a spiritual family. A family has a mother and father. In monastic language the spiritual father is called an abbot; the spiritual mother is called an abbess. We also have older brothers and sisters who are called elders, and the first in leadership status among the elders is called a prior. These words all come from family usage and mean that we are a spiritual family in Christ and the church. We are also part of the greater human family within creation itself. The monastic family is a microcosm of them all.

The qualities of the abbot are really qualities for all of us. The abbot holds the place of Christ in the monastery so that we might learn to see Jesus in everyone and become more like Christ ourselves. We are all Christians, or "like Christ," and every human being bears the image of God. All creation bears his traces. When we learn to find Christ in the abbot, we are just beginning to learn how to find Jesus in everyone and in everything.

The abbot teaches the way of God through word and example. We are also to teach not just with words but also with the example of our life. Words are easy. Living is hard. If our life does not speak, then our words are empty. If we do not live like Jesus, then speaking the words of Jesus will not convince anyone about Jesus. Words must flow from life; then words can lead back to life.

The abbot's teaching is adapted to each person individually. He is to treat all equally but not identically. Unity does not mean absolute uniformity. Truth must be applied with love, and love must be guided by truth. One without the other is incomplete and often imbalanced. Some are meek and some are strong-willed. A harsh measure will crush the meek and a weak measure will have no effect on the strong-willed. Though the end does not always justify the means, the final result, not the means, is the point. It takes wisdom to know the difference.

Abbots must deal with business in the temporal world but must be rooted in the spiritual. They must first be persons of prayer. We must do the same. Jesus calls us to be in the world but not of the world. Our first work is prayer. Then our action will be life-giving to others. In turn, it enriches us too. Prayer overflows into action, and action leads back to prayer. Then our whole life becomes a prayer. Action not rooted in prayer and meditation is incomplete and does not bear lasting fruit.

The qualities of the abbot are for all of us. We can all learn how to live and apply the teaching of Jesus wisely in order to build up our own earthly families, local churches, and faith communities as spiritual families in Christ. We can know wisdom from a life of meditation and prayer and lead everyone back to know God in Christ through deeper prayer and meditation. These qualities of the abbot help us all to be one spiritual family and a blessing of God for all. It is a blessing of St. Benedict.

## Chapter 3

## Calling the Brothers and Sisters for Counsel

The abbot is the spiritual father of the community. The buck stops with the abbot, and he takes final responsibility for the monastery. But the abbot makes few decisions alone. The entire community assists in the more important matters. Less important ones are decided between the abbot and a council of elders.

Scripture says that wisdom is found in the council of many. Pastors have pastoral councils, and bishops have councils of clergy and laity to help them hear the voice of God. Even the pope has a curia and must listen to the sense of the faithful before he speaks to and for them in God's name. The monastery has a chapter and councils of elders who assist the abbot in his leadership duties. Without them the abbot is easily overwhelmed.

Scripture and tradition are filled with examples of individuals from the lowliest to the highest of every state of life who prophetically stood up against the crowd to proclaim God's word. This takes courage and great wisdom. Abbots and members must sometimes do the same.

The voice of God can speak through anyone. That is why the abbot listens not only to the older and more experienced monks but also the newest and youngest novices. St. Francis said that he would follow a novice of one hour who spoke God's word to him! Sometimes we need to hear the voice of the newcomer who still has a fresh view of some of the things we have come to accept but simply do not work.

We speak God's word to one another with humility. We treat others as Christ and speak to them as we would to Jesus himself. He is in all of us. We speak only after listening and praying in silence. We must be more willing to learn than to teach, more willing to follow than to lead. Only then can we safely speak. This is especially true for novices but must first be first exemplified by the older monks.

We learn to share humbly and respectfully with each other. The saints say that humility is just the truth. Compared to the infinite wisdom of God, we know very little. That is the truth. We share in God, but we are not God. So we are always humble before others who also bear the image of God.

There is a time for everyone to speak in order for the spiritual family to prosper. False silence is a community killer. It oppresses spirits. It breeds discontent and gossip. Then the community is as good as dead. So we must speak at the right time and in the right way. We are not confrontational, course, or rude. We do not shout, interrupt, or belittle, especially with leaders. We speak the truth in love. The good spiritual leader calls the members together for counsel and listens most seriously. Then the leader can be a blessing to the community and the community to the leader. Then the community can be a blessing to the entire church and world! It is a blessing of St. Benedict.

## Chapter 4

# The Tools for Good Works

This chapter is predominantly a string of Scripture quotes that address our life in Christ. Our entire way of life must be based on Sacred Scripture. The New Testament is the earliest written record of the teaching of the apostles chosen by Jesus and their immediate disciples and successors. It is the measuring stick, or canon, by which we measure all else in the church. As St. Jerome said, "Ignorance of Scripture is ignorance of Christ."

At first these quotes seem fairly scattered and random. But there is a logic and flow to them. They deal with external issues, and then flow inward and back out. Beginning with the basics to love God, they jump almost immediately to nonresistance in attitude and action. Ascetical self-mortification and self-control are linked to greater charity and peacefulness with friend and foe alike that can only flow from a spirit and soul of deep peace. Classical means such as sacred reading, prayer, and confession of sin lead to a renunciation of the old self-will and a life of love with everyone. At first a bit off-putting by the sheer number in this list, once really prayed and slowly pondered they become a most beautiful means of aiding our journey inward to God, and outward to help others on a similar journey.

All of us are called to make this journey. Pondering these Scriptures as tools of the spiritual craft, we make the journey with Christ inward. And once the inside is renewed in him, we journey outward and forward to touch everyone with the beauty of what he has crafted from our life.

We become his work of art. What is beautiful from this wide range of Scriptures is the centrality of the teaching of Jesus' Sermon on the Mount that permeates the whole. The rough things of monastic asceticism end in the gentle peace of Jesus.

The monastery is the workshop where the tools listed in chapter 4 are practiced and used; it requires both enclosure and stability. It requires focus. We cannot leave the workshop too frequently or we will never finish the task. We will get distracted. We must remain in the workshop until the task is done. That takes a lifetime.

Likewise, we might feel compelled to flit about from one spiritual movement to another, from one parish to another, from one monastery to another. We might feel drawn to go out and minister when we are enclosed in prayer and want to go back to prayer when in ministry. We might want solitude when in community or community when in solitude. This rhythm is sometimes appropriate as an integrated call of prayer and action but not as a distracted state of mind. We must resist these temptations to instability. Be still. Meditate and pray. Then work and work well. We must learn to hunker down and see things through to their end if we are to reap the benefits and blessings of these tools. We must patiently practice before we can build. And when we build, we must finish what we start. Otherwise it does not bear lasting spiritual fruit. Bear fruit. Be a blessing. Use these scriptural tools for good works as a blessing of St. Benedict.

## Chapter 5

# Obedience

The heart of both the Christian faith and monastic life is letting go of the old self and being born again as a new person in Jesus Christ. In the Rule of St. Benedict this is found in letting go of self-will through obedience.

Many think of obedience in negative terms of restricting individual freedom and such. This is not really what obedience is about. Instead, it is about liberating us from the ego attachments of pride and self-will. This sets us free for love, joy, and peace in all situations. Obedience makes us new and sets us free. It makes us happy, not sad.

The heart of obedience is listening. To listen we must be silent and still. Then we can hear and know what to say and how to act. To be obedient is to be a person of humble and quiet meditation and contemplative prayer in all things. It makes our whole life a prayer and the entire world a monastery.

Obedience also functions externally. Even in meditation we still the body and breath. This is physical. Plus, the function of a family, business, or monastery requires that we all sacrifice a bit of ourselves to work together externally for a greater common good. Obedience benefits everyone in the end.

But this is not mere military obedience. It is a supernatural obedience. By letting go of ego attachments and seeing Jesus clearly in obedience, we can follow with love and joy in Jesus. When ego attachments are relinquished we are free and happy even when we do not get what we want. That is why Benedict requires that monastic obedience be quick and without grumbling if it is to be pleasing to God. It is about following Jesus everywhere and in all things, the good and bad alike.

Benedictine obedience is not done out of mere compulsion or religious law. It is done out of love. "It is love that impels [us]" (RB 5.10). It is about loving Jesus. By loving we share in the divine nature, even as he shared in our humanity. We also become more humane. Monasteries are places where heaven comes to earth, and monastics find heaven in earthly relationships and work. Love sacrifices itself for another and creates new life in the process. Monasteries are places where we live not for ourselves but for God and others.

Obedience is incarnational. It is lived out in a very real and tangible way, "choosing to live in monasteries and to have an abbot over them." This is not some kind of fluffy obedience. It has feet that are placed firmly on the ground so that the spirit might soar unhindered to heaven. Monasteries are very real places, and abbots are very real people. All the same challenges of saints and sinners are found here.

We also live out obedience in the realities of life. We all have families and jobs, as well as churches, faith communities, and ministries. Some of us live in monasteries. We like some things and dislike others. Each of these presents opportunities for a monastic obedience so all can be free in everything. It is a blessing of St. Benedict.

## Chapter 6

# Silence and Restraint of Speech

It is only when we learn how to be silent that words can be spoken. Words flow best from silence, for in silence we hear the Word. Occasionally, this Word is best spoken through silence. It is sometimes too big for the human tongue and can only be spoken in the Spirit.

In silence we learn how to hear between the words. It is there that we hear the Spirit. When we learn to hear the silence between the words, then we learn to hear the silence in every word. We hear the Spirit behind the Word.

The Rule quotes the Scripture that in many words sin is not lacking. When we do not discipline our speech, we often end up saying too much, and when we say too much, we usually say things we don't need to say. These words often fall into gossip and even slander. Silence means restraining words that are sinful.

We also restrain words that are good but not really necessary. We do not always have to speak and are to speak the right thing rightly. This is an art that flows from silence. If we are satisfied with silence, then we may safely speak. Otherwise we are usually speaking from our own egotistical need to be noticed.

Sometimes we lose spiritual joy by telling superficial or sarcastic jokes. Benedict advocates a deeper joy. Modern monks may share wholesome jokes that are fun and uplifting to everyone, but hurtful or superficial jokes and laughter cheapen the deeper joy of the spiritual soul. We do not speak just to make others laugh and to draw attention to ourselves. That is the ego talking.

Nevertheless, silence is not an escape from the duty to speak when asked to share. Silence implies consent. We are not silent in the presence of evil. Jesus is the Word Incarnate. We share in his continuing incarnation in the church, but we share humbly as learners, not as masters. If we are afraid of humble silence, then we must beware of speaking. But if we are afraid to speak humbly at the right time and place, then we must beware of silence. That too can be pride.

It is best to learn this way of silence under a wise abbot or elder. This way is a great tool to gauge the authenticity of our words. It is the superior who gives us permission to speak. Otherwise we should remain silent. And this permission is rarely given, even to mature monks. We are all too easily tempted to talkativeness.

In every monastery there are places and times for greater silence. The same can be true in our homes. Even children have a natural disposition to restful silence when guided by a parent or leader who has a silent and peaceful heart. Scripture implies that silence is difficult but is the essential element of wisdom. When silent, we often think we will burst if we cannot speak. But we will not. Silence makes us better listeners and proclaimers of the Word. And sometimes we speak the most profound blessing by sacred silence. It is a blessing of St. Benedict.

# Chapter 7
# Humility

This is the longest chapter in the Rule and ends the treatment of its basic spiritual heart. It is quite challenging to the modern reader but is also quite beautiful when rightly understood. Humility literally means being brought to the earth. It is grounding our whole being by being firmly rooted in Christ. Only then can the branches of our life reach high to the heavens and accomplish great things for God.

We cannot do great things for God and others unless we begin with humility, but if we embrace humility only to do great things, we are not really humble. If we think we are humble, then we are not. If we want to be noticed for our humility, then we are still filled with pride.

Humility can be learned. Jesus teaches us the way. He says to take the lowest place, not the highest; seek to serve and not be served. These are the ways of Jesus who came not to be served but to serve and to lay down his own life so many might truly live. Even the greatest master remains but a learner of the way of humility.

The Rule also teaches us twelve steps in learning humility. They are likened to rungs on a ladder leading to heaven. They take us through several general motions. The first is humility before God. Then we learn humility through others, beginning with our religious leaders and branching out to the community we live with. At first, the way is difficult and grates against our old self. After many years, it becomes a kind of second nature in all that we do as we are fully reborn in Christ. But it cannot be learned any other way. It takes time but is well worth the effort.

Specifically the steps of humility are:

- Fear, awe, and wonder before God
- Letting go of the old self-will
- Obedience to an abbot
- Obedience with joy, even in difficult things
- Voluntary revelation of one's thoughts to a trusted abbot (not just sins as in sacramental confession)
- Being content with lowliness and poverty in Christ
- Finding joy in the gifts of others before having our own gifts noticed and rewarded
- Doing only what is part of the common life of the monks and superiors of our monastery
- Sacred silence
- Refraining from unhealthy laughter
- Speaking gently
- Being humble in every aspect of our life

We begin with the fear of God but end in a perfect love that casts out all fear. We begin with discipline in specific things but end in liberating freedom in all things. We begin with some hard work and even some sorrow but end in ease of spirit and perfect joy!

Humility returns us to what was originally natural as creatures of God. It is a supernatural naturalness. Bernard of Clairvaux says that a humble person can be seen even in the way they walk. Those who parade are not humble, nor are those who are artificially meek. The humble person walks selflessly with an unhurried ease that gets to the destination faster than anyone else! Natural humility is a blessing to everyone. It also becomes a blessing for us as well as we begin to walk everywhere in perfect peace. It is a blessing of St. Benedict.

Chapters 8–20

# The Work of God, the Divine Office

"Nothing is to be preferred to the Work of God" (43.3). We meet God in prayer and overflow from prayer into action. Monks specialize in prayer and community. As early monasteries were for hermits and cenobites, monastic prayer was both private and public, individual and in common. While recognizing that God is present everywhere, the Rule says that he is especially present during the Work of God, praying the Psalter and Scriptures in common. Nothing in the monastery is to be preferred to the Work of God in common prayer. All activity revolves around it and finds direction and strength from it.

The chapters on the Work of God make up over 10 percent of the entire Rule. With its legislative lists of psalms for each office, it is not immediately easy to see the spirituality of those chapters, but if we look deeper they have much to teach us.

Benedict was the great harmonizer. He wove the monastic strands of the past into one strong cord. He moderated the excesses into a livable whole. This is found in his treatment of the Work of God. We must also build on what has come before while moving into the future. We cannot ignore or go back into the past.

The Psalter forms the praying heart of the church. The monks prayed it as well. The cathedrals prayed the psalms thematically, not in order as the early monks did. The cathedral tradition sanctified certain hours of the day, and the monastic tradition emphasized ceaseless meditation throughout the day. The Rule harmonizes these traditions in a creative way that worked best for Benedict's communities. Monastics and the church throughout history also recognized the needs of each local monastery and person within the practice of the greater monastic tradition and church universal.

Benedict also adapted the monastic cycle to fit the seasons. The winter days were shorter and the summer days longer, so the Office reflects that rhythm. The time and length of each Office reflect the season. One of the unique gifts of the Rule is this capacity to harmonize, integrate, and adapt without losing specific sacrifice, practical application, or communion with the entire church and monastic traditions. We must also adapt our prayer to the seasons of our life.

While the Psalter was a formulated written prayer, there were also times for silence and spontaneous prayers during the Work of God. Liturgical law alone does not save us. We need the form of liturgy and the freedom of the Spirit to be fully alive in Christ. The spontaneous prayers after each psalm were to be kept short so that silence would not be abused.

The Rule emphasizes the Work of God as the primary expression of monastic common worship. It never explicitly defines the Mass and Communion. It does explicitly mention priests. But the Eucharist was an important part of the earlier monastic tradition. The Eucharist was no doubt a part of their weekly common worship.

The Work of God is presided over by the local abbot, who was probably a layperson originally. Priests presided only at Mass. The monastic Office is a great sign of hope for the church as we rediscover the important and unique roles of the laity and the clergy and the role of the Liturgy of the Hours in the prayer of the church.

After the Eucharist the most important ongoing prayer of the Catholic Church is the Liturgy of the Hours. The church encourages us all to discover its riches and use it in our daily prayer whenever we can. The monastic Work of God takes us beyond individual prayer to the prayer of a local community or entire monastic congregation. The Roman Liturgy of the Hours takes us beyond the prayer of a monastic community to the prayer of the Latin Rite. Both are great ways to expand our private and public prayers beyond private devotions and Mass in a way that brings greater life to both. It is one of the blessings of St. Benedict.

## Chapter 13
## Time and Character of the Offices

As we have already noted, the first monks prayed all 150 psalms daily in biblical order as an ongoing meditation. The cathedral tradition prayed them thematically to consecrate specific hours of the day around the life of Christ. By the time of Benedict these two had intertwined. But it was still evolving, so each region and monastery developed its own liturgical cycle for praying the Work of God.

Benedict devotes an enormous amount of space to the specific time and psalms of each Office or prayer hour. The community is to go through all 150 psalms in a weekly cycle and adapt the times to the liturgical and natural seasons of the year. These times are traditionally given Latin names but have been anglicized in recent years. Out of the eight, Morning and Evening Prayer are the two most important offices, often called the "hinges" of the monastic day. This is also true in the Roman Liturgy of the Hours of the church.

Matins, or what the Rule calls "Vigils," is the hour that is prayed after eight hours of sleep at around two or three o'clock in the morning. The nature of this hour of prayer is watching with God in the quiet hours of the night before dawn. It is the longest office and includes extended and beautiful biblical, patristic, and monastic readings for reflection. Prime is the brief "first" hour that is usually just prior to the longer Lauds, or Morning Prayer. Their character is one of greeting with praise and thanksgiving a new day to love and serve God, all people, and creation. Terce (third hour; nine o'clock in the morning), Sext (sixth hour; noon), and None (ninth hour; three o'clock in the afternoon) are the short day hours now called Midmorning, Noon, and Midafternoon Prayer, respectively. Vespers is Evening Prayer. It brings the main work and prayer of the day to a close and thanks God for them. Vespers was often the most solemn of the Offices in Catholic tradition. Compline is Night Prayer and brings the entire day to a close before retiring. It usually includes a brief examination of conscience to cleanse the soul before sleep and to ready the monk if he or she dies in the night. Compline focuses the last thoughts of the mind on God and helps the monastic drift off to peaceful sleep in Christ.

These Offices consecrate the day by pausing at set hours with the rest of the community and the church to reflect on God through the psalms at times significant to Jewish tradition and the life of Jesus. By stopping at particular hours, we are reminded to pray without ceasing at all hours of the day. Morning and Evening Prayer are the two most important, and we all do well to at least pray these.

The autonomy of the Benedictine Office and each monastery also reminds us that the monastic life is not identical with the diocesan church but is a microcosm and a supporter of the larger church universal. We too are individuals within a larger community of faith. Like the Office, we are also developing throughout our life in Christ. This is a great lesson and blessing from Benedict.

Chapter 21

# The Deans of the Monastery

I have a rather negative image of a dean, probably because many of us feared being sent to the dean's office in high school! But in monastic usage the dean is a good person. The dean is the leader of small groups of ten or so in a larger community so that real personal relationships in Christ can be fostered, formed, and maintained. This system is also where we get the church's arrangement of "deaneries" in each diocese.

Benedict got this notion of deans from a monastic tradition that goes all the way back to the first generation of Christian monks. St. Pachomius's monasteries were based on *koinonia*, or communion and fellowship, and could be quite large, some say in the thousands, but at least hundreds is certain. Deaneries broke the larger community down into smaller groups of ten or so, according to occupation. A dean led each household, which lived together in their rather large monastic village. They prayed at least one common prayer service together in each house daily. Other services were prayed in the church.

Benedict drops aspects of the Pachomian arrangement to adapt it to his monasteries, but he keeps the basic idea. Tradition tells us that the size of the Benedictine monastery of the first generation was around twelve monks, but they could apparently get much larger and eventually did. A large community gives a great sense of stability, but it is not always good for relationships based on the example of Jesus and the apostles. Something smaller is necessary. The deanery and deans are a good way to break larger communities into small groups in a more Christlike way.

The deans are genuine spiritual leaders to the monks in their care. They are to help carry some of the weight of the abbot's pastoral and administrative burdens. But they do not replace the abbot. The abbot delegates his authority to them. The dean brings the love of the abbot to each monk in a personal way. If the dean ever gets puffed up by or proud of his authority or challenges the abbot's authority, he is corrected a few times. But if he does not change, he has his authority taken from him in order to teach him the humility he asks of others. The same is true of the prior, who the Rule only cautiously allows for.

Many new monastic communities try to stay smaller for this reason. But they grow. Smaller groups and shared leadership responsibility are necessary when they grow. Integrated communities usually have leaders for each expression—celibate men and women, singles who can marry, and monastic families—as well as department heads. Even parishes break into smaller faith-sharing and ministry groups in order to be effective in sharing Jesus with each other and the world.

Benedict wisely accommodates this genuine spiritual and pastoral need in his monasteries. He reminds us that in addition to the universal, diocesan, or local church, we also need to be part of a small faith community to fully enjoy the riches of the gospel of Jesus. It is one of the often-overlooked blessings of St. Benedict.

## Chapter 22

# The Sleeping Arrangements of the Monks

Related to the chapter on the deans are the housing and sleeping arrangements for the monks. The reason for this relation comes from monastic history. In Pachomius's monasteries each group had its own house. In Benedict's monasteries all the monks slept in separate beds but in one common dormitory in groups of ten or twenty. Older monks were dispersed among them to maintain discipline and order.

In Europe in those days it was uncommon for average people to have their own bedrooms. Families slept in one room. It was a luxury even for parents to have their own private room. Monasteries were a spiritual family and did pretty much the same thing. Even in recent times monks slept in common dormitories in beds that had little partitions around them. This was considered their "cell," an often-enclosed inner room in a temple where heaven came to earth in the presence of a deity. By our modern standards nothing was terribly private in Benedict's cenobitical monasteries.

The hermitage was considered special. Hermits had their own cells, usually in a small, separate apartment or cottage in the larger monastic complex. But this was considered a sacrifice of solitude due to the more communal orientation of society in those days. Real Christian solitude is no escape from community.

A light was kept burning in the monk's dormitory at night. They also slept fully clothed. This was to keep them ready to rise to meet Jesus in prayer at Vigils around two or three o'clock in the morning after eight hours of sleep. It was also to keep monks from wandering to one another's cells to gossip or to sin sexually. Few people actually had nightclothes in those days. The average person slept in regular clothes and used his cloak as a cover. The monks were no different.

Today most Benedictine monasteries allow for separate cells or rooms in a dormitory much like in colleges and universities. Our generation is accustomed to having private rooms in family houses. Modern monasteries do the same.

We all need a balance of solitude and community. The cell is where we find solitude, and the other monastic areas are where we find community. The cell is for private prayer and spiritual reading, or *lectio*. The monastic church is for common prayer and meditation, the refectory for common meals, and workplaces for common work.

We keep our cells free of clutter and clean so as to always be ready for the coming of Christ in *lectio* and prayer. We must also find a balance between work and rest but always be ready to rise to meet Jesus at Vigils even if he comes in the middle of the night. We also do well to take appropriate precautions against sexual sin and gossip. We do not normally meet visitors or monastics in our cells. We help remove sin by removing the occasion for sin.

Though seemingly insignificant, even this little chapter can extend one of the blessings of Benedict.

Chapters 23–28

# Monastic Excommunication

We would like to think that things always go well for monks in monasteries dedicated to God. But they do not. Monasteries are places made up of very ordinary people who have made an extraordinary commitment. So, good monasteries must make provision for correction and forgiveness when offenses are committed.

In these chapters and others the Rule devotes another large portion of its contents to excommunication for offenses against the community and God. To be excommunicated means to be excluded from full participation in a community dedicated to God. At best, it is a kind of religious "time out." It is for our good and not our harm. It teaches us that our actions affect others, and there are community consequences for them.

The Rule describes various ways to apply this discipline. The discipline is in proportion to the offense. For more serious offenses the monk is kept from his normal place in church or at table. It is a symbol that his behavior has already spiritually done what is being symbolized. Lesser offenses are given proportionally lesser measures that are not specifically mentioned. But they all symbolize the notion of cause and effect. In more extreme cases a monk can receive the accepted corporal punishment of the day. It is the last attempt before the monk is asked to leave the monastery. For us this seems most extreme and is unacceptable, but for them it was an accepted form of correction and not considered unloving. It was a last effort of love to save a soul from sin. For us today it would not be unlike going for professional help when all other pastoral counseling had failed.

Monks may not associate with the excommunicated. The treatment of the offending monk must be left to the healing remedy of the abbot or his delegates. To intrude on the process can cause unintended harm. We may want to check in on the monk, but it may cause him more harm than good. We do not intrude. But the abbot is not to leave the excommunicated in solitary sorrow either. That might be too much to bear. He discreetly sends wise older monks to check up on the offending monk and offer help and encouragement. The point is not to punish but to heal.

Yet, some are asked to leave after it becomes obvious that they will not willingly change and return to the full spiritual life of the monastic community. This is always difficult but must be done for the sake of the greater good of the community. Like amputating a limb, it is difficult when done but saves a life in the process.

When a monk repents he must make satisfaction or show some real signs of repentance and change. This is usually done publicly by kneeling before the abbot or the community and asking pardon. If a person is willing to do this, he is usually serious. If not, he is only saying words. But life change is the real test.

After excommunication and satisfaction the monk receives public forgiveness. This closes the matter once and for all. After this there can be no more healthy mention of it. The abbot usually pronounces it, but all brothers do so on some occasions. We all participate in forgiveness. There can be no residual judgment or resentment afterward. That is the only way a community can stay healthy.

Today these protocols are interpreted and applied in various ways that respect the basic human rights of individuals and the good of communities. But the principle of those with authority applying public and private healing measures for offenses and personal responsibility for actions remain.

This rather uncomfortable section of the Rule teaches us that there are consequences for our actions. When we behave as if we were not in community, we actually excommunicate ourselves from it. These measures only bring it to light. Learning to take responsibility for our actions is a difficult and sometimes embarrassing lesson, especially in the close relationships of a monastic community or family. Nevertheless, it is a lesson that, if embraced, becomes a blessing that lasts for life. It is one of the blessings of St. Benedict.

Chapter 29

# Readmission of Brothers Who Leave the Monastery

Despite our best efforts to help others who have problems in community, we do not always succeed. Sometimes it is best if they leave the monastery and return to secular life. There they can test if it is better suited to them.

Once they have left, they sometimes wonder if they have not made a mistake. They might want to return. This is a real test for the community. Often the circumstances around their leaving were not pleasant. When a person leaves or is dismissed, both sides sometimes want to find fault to make it seem "right." This causes hurt feelings. Regardless of whether a person ends up returning, finding forgiveness is essential for the community and the individual if genuine growth in Jesus is to continue unimpeded. Forgiveness is nonnegotiable for the real Christian.

Sometimes they want to return because they couldn't make it outside the monastery and see it as a place of security. But they have not really changed. Maybe it is apparent to the community and not to the individual that they are simply not cut out for monastic community life. Sometimes they might eventually return, but it is too soon for them to have really healed and tested life outside the community. It is difficult for a community to offer true forgiveness yet still deny them the chance to return in these cases, but it must be done. It is for the greater good and for the sake of their well-being as well as the community's. This is a difficult call.

It takes real discernment to sort this out. It is essential to respond without self-interest and with a truly loving heart born of the letting go of self-will through the cross of Christ. We cannot deny their return just because it will be inconvenient. That remains self-serving and egocentric and cannot be called Christian.

It is a great joy when some return to the monastery if everyone discerns that it is right. It allows us to put feet to our forgiveness for past faults and helps the monastery continue in Christlike love. It is a win-win situation and brings the whole community great joy.

Benedict recommends allowing this process up to three times, though it is always the community's call as to whether to allow it at all. After three times if it still does not work out, they should not be allowed to return. We all must eventually make a vocational decision and stick with it. There can be no further dallying. Love is a decision, and it is for life.

The Rule is a practical guide helping to discern the will of God when a person wants to return to a particular monastery. It is also helpful in families. It is filled with love and forgiveness. But it also has its feet planted firmly on the ground of daily community life. It is difficult to offer forgiveness, and it is difficult to practice tough love. Families and monasteries need both. The Rule helps us find the wisdom to know when to do either. It is one of the blessings of St. Benedict.

Chapter 30

# Children and the Manner of Reproving Boys

People are often surprised by the mention of children in the Rule of St. Benedict, but children had become an important part of monastic culture by the time of Benedict. They remained so for centuries.

Wealthy parents often donated their later-born children as oblates, or "oblations," so that they could be trained in the monastery. They often went on to become monastic or secular priests, abbots, and bishops instead of secular lords like the firstborn. Poorer families donated children as well. They went on to become lay monastics who helped maintain the monasteries. All things considered, it was a very good life, and monasteries, the church, and society in general profited by the arrangement. Girls went through a similar process with nuns.

This developed into the Benedictine ministry of education in places like the United States. Ranging from elementary to university levels, Benedictine monks and sisters educated not only future monks, nuns, and clerics but also some of the future leaders of our culture. The blessing to our country is beyond estimation.

Today there is a new development. The New Monastics often live in integrated monasteries where traditional celibate monks and sisters, singles who can marry, and families with or without children all live together in a way that retains the integrity of each one's state of life. Children are often a vital and vibrant part of these integrated monasteries. The mention of children in the Rule of Benedict is most helpful to these new integrated expressions.

The Rule says that children participate in the monastic life but in a way appropriate to their age and strength. They cannot be expected to participate as fully as adults. They are not expected to fast, work, or pray with the same intensity of time or energy. Although they are disciplined, they are not disciplined as adults.

In integrated monasteries children learn the values of religion, community, and family in a healthy and complete way that our society is quickly losing. They are insulated but not isolated. The community strengthens the quickly eroding family unit with mutual support, and the families enrich the community. The community becomes a wonderful extended family of spiritual grandparents, aunts, and uncles who enrich the children with experience. Children also keep celibates young at heart as signs of hope for the future. Some in the church believe that new monastics and clerics will come from the children of family monastics where the family is being strengthened in the faith. Time will tell.

The Rule of St. Benedict provides a guideline that is balanced, tested, and true as we face this new phenomenon. Even for raising children in the modern world the Rule provides an ancient blessing from St. Benedict.

## Chapter 31

## The Cellarer

Like Jesus and the church, monasteries are "in the world but not of the world." Jesus was the Word Incarnate, or "made flesh." The spiritual world of the monastery must be lived in the world of material reality as well. And these two worlds must be harmonized to bring peace to the monks and the world in which the monastery finds itself.

The cellarer is the daily overseer of the material side of the monastery. He makes sure that everyone has what they truly need for personal and communal use without giving into consumerism or worldliness. It is a most important role.

If the material needs of the monastery are not fairly accommodated for, then discontent settles in. Then the things of the spirit are disrupted. The cellarer makes sure that all runs smoothly on a daily basis.

The key is to meet the genuine needs of all without showing favoritism to any. The cellarer is not to annoy the brothers but to care for them. The sick, the weak, and children are given special consideration. But he must also know when to deny an unreasonable request, or one that he simply does not have the means to fulfill. He does this without losing his humility or peace of soul. He should not be angry, stingy, or controlling. That spreads unrest in a monastery.

This takes maturity on the part of the cellarer. Besides the abbot, he is a true spiritual father to all. He is to have most of the same qualities of the abbot, without usurping the abbot's authority. This description is significant.

Most importantly, he is to be a man of the Spirit. The administration of temporal goods is not to make him carnal or worldly. He brings the harmony of heaven to earth and the creativity of the Creator to creation beginning in the monastery itself.

When this happens all the goods of the monastery are treated as reverently as "sacred vessels of the altar." This is one of the most profound sayings in the Rule. Starting with the cellarer, a true incarnational spirituality permeates the entire monastery. It becomes an altar for God, and the monastic community becomes a eucharist where Jesus is continually offered as a thanksgiving of divine love for the sake of the world.

Today most monasteries do not use the title "cellarer." We have administrators, department heads, bookkeepers, and such. But the meaning is the same for all. They must be good followers of Jesus and the abbot before they can lead. They must be humble before they can direct others and people of the Spirit before they can oversee material goods.

The same is true of any monastic family or those in the world. We must all deal with the Spirit and the flesh in order to experience and bring the Incarnate Word into this world. Benedict had the wisdom to understand and accommodate this in his monasteries. It is one of his blessings for us today.

Chapter 32

# The Tools and Goods of the Monastery

We have already heard that we are to treat the tools of the monastery as we would the sacred vessels of the altar. That alone is a revolutionary concept for most of us today. It sacramentalizes our entire way of life personally and communally. It makes all things sacred. The monastery is the school where we learn how to do this. This chapter is a brief follow-up to that more sweeping and grand statement.

How? Is there some esoteric secret? I am afraid not. Simply put, Benedict says that we are to keep an inventory of all the tools, clothes, and such and that they are to be checked by the leaders the abbot delegates to take care of them. We take care of things. That's all. At the Hermitage we have found that when everyone owns everything, no one takes responsibility for anything unless it is specifically assigned. When asked where a tool or item is, "I don't know" is a very common answer. We say, "'I don't know' doesn't live here!" The irony is that the same item will sometimes mysteriously reappear after it is asked about in a community meeting. Obviously, somebody knew! Monasteries are most ordinary and human places indeed!

The inventory was also kept because monks rotated work positions throughout the monastery. Modern monasteries also experience a turnover of personnel due to the transience of Western society. Members come and go, even after profession. When they go, the ones who stay have to pick up the pieces and carry on. That can be most disturbing if an inventory and proper records are not kept. Without them we would always be starting from scratch.

But this does not always happen, even when emphasized again and again. We all "amen" the ideas of monastic life and are attracted to them, or we would not have come to the monastery in the first place. But once we arrive the zeal often fades, and we drift back into old irresponsible patterns that haunted us in the secular world. We can even inflict them on everyone else in the monastery as well.

That is why the Rule speaks of discipline again in this context. Basically the idea is learning consequences for good or bad actions. Today when we lose or damage things, we must find a way to repair or replace them. When we show up late for work due to negligence, we must stay longer after work to pick up the slack we left for others. We all affect one another. The ancient discipline of Benedict teaches us this lesson in a society that seems to have lost that understanding.

Ironically, we adults must relearn these lessons that were once the basic stuff of what was taught to children. Today we adults have often not learned them, so we pass that dysfunction on to the next generation. Perhaps because our parents tried to save us from the dire poverty of the Great Depression they met our every need and want. But it created a generation with a sense of entitlement, thinking that we were owed everything without really having to work or take responsibility for anything. The Rule moderately and patiently corrects that sin and abuse. It is one of blessings of St. Benedict for our time.

## Chapter 33

# Private Ownership and Monks

The Rule says that private ownership is a grave evil that must be uprooted and removed from the monastery above all else! It is some of the strongest language used anywhere in the Rule. Why? Probably because it was so common. It is still very common today and is one of the main reasons why the spiritual zeal of monks often cools and entire monasteries become lukewarm. It is an indicator of our selfless response, or lack thereof, to the poor Christ and our brother and sister monastics.

Jesus asks us to renounce everything to follow him, not because creation is bad, but because we tend to use it badly. A clean break with past patterns is usually necessary to help establish new ones. The celibates and the families of the early church in Jerusalem held all things in common so that there was no one in need among them (Acts 4:32). The early monks did the same thing. The oft-repeated quote from Evagrius says, "Renounce all to gain everything."

In our integrated monastery we recognize that those in different states of life live this out differently. Celibates give up all private possessions. Singles often need private possessions due to various responsibilities, and families need them for their spouses and children. But even they usually work at the monastery, so common ownership is the normal experience for all of us. Our domestic members who live in the secular world have the right to private property but also the privilege to share with those in need.

Even celibates are not identical in how this gospel poverty is lived out. In the old days monks were usually forbidden mementos or gifts from family and friends. Today we are less strict but do not allow it when it creates envy, inequality, or a return to the consumerism or worldliness that is contrary to monastic life itself. Celibates are given what they need for a craft that accompanies prayer in their cells, but they do not own it. Otherwise very little is really needed.

This poverty also creates a sense of childlikeness that is called blessed by Jesus. Dependence on the abbot or abbess in the monastery for all material things helps us to remember that we are dependent on God for everything on earth. We are not codependent; rather, we are interdependent. This should not make us childish or irresponsible. True childlikeness makes us better stewards of God's many gifts. Childlikeness is the way to maturity and wisdom, not immaturity and childishness.

As with the last chapter, discipline is mentioned if the monk fails in living out this virtue. It is intended as an aid, not in a punitive spirit, but rather an instructive one.

In a modern world where rampant consumerism and gross inequality between the rich and the poor is so evident, this rule against private ownership is a great blessing. It is a way in which the monastery becomes an image of heaven on earth. Every Christian home and parish can become a little monastery as well. It is not about what we cannot have but rather about what we get to share so that we all have what we need in the love of God though Jesus. It is a blessing of St. Benedict.

## Chapter 34

## Distribution of Goods

This chapter is a practical application of the previous one about private ownership. It demonstrates the Rule's ability to take spiritual principles and pastoral applications of Scripture and apply them to a current situation in tangible ways.

Following Acts 4 from the last chapter, it completes the notion of common ownership by truly meeting individuals' needs. The point is not to deprive monks of their legitimate needs but to meet them while disciplining the monks from indulging their wants. God wants to meet our needs and even gives us some of our wants. He loves us. But habitually indulging our wants steals from the needy and addicts us to consumerism. Community of goods through liberating obedience is a wonderful but sometimes challenging cure.

We do not show favoritism but do accommodate for weakness. We seek unity but not uniformity. All are treated equally but not identically. This notion goes back to the Rule of St. Augustine and the teaching of the Desert Fathers. The Fathers say that a senator who gave up many riches might still seem to have more, but the monk from a poor background who seems to have less may not have actually given up as much. We should not judge.

Those who are weak need more, and those who are strong need less. The weak thank God that their needs are met, and the strong thank God that they can make sacrifices. There is no pride in either. The weak who receive more are not to be proud because of their abundance, and those who are strong should not be ashamed of their poverty. We all share in the poverty of Christ. It is a poverty born of love. Those who sacrifice more should rejoice that they can give in the love of Jesus, and those who receive should rejoice in that love as well.

Not to meet needs when we have the means to do so is injustice. To sacrifice our wants for God and others is love. The Rule helps us to know the difference.

The Rule then warns of a theme we have heard before: grumbling. It is a sure killer of community morale and simply cannot be allowed. We either raise each other up or push each other down. Our attitudes affect our brothers and sisters. Grumbling brings everyone down. Those who grumble are still operating on ego. The ego is attached to the flesh, the emotions, or its own ideas. When it does not get what it wants, it grumbles. When we bring our ego attachment to the cross through obedience, we stop grumbling and complaining. We learn how to share our needs, wants, and opinions freely in love and respect because we are no longer attached to them through our ego. When they are satisfied, we can rejoice. Needs are almost always met. Some wants are not. And not everyone agrees with our opinions about this or that. When we do not get these unnecessary things, we are content. When we embrace the poverty of Jesus, we are always and everywhere at peace.

This is one of the blessings of the Rule of St. Benedict.

## Chapter 35

# Kitchen Servers of the Week

It was once said to hopeful brides that "The way to a man's heart is through his stomach." In the military a good meal makes for a happier soldier.

It also true of monasteries. After the church, the refectory and the kitchen are perhaps the most important places in the monastery. If you do not believe how important they are, just wait until the cook does a poor job a few days in a row! Monks can get most unhappy when the meager fare of a monastery is not well prepared.

Everyone shares in kitchen duty. Only the abbot and those engaged in other important business do not participate, but even they did for quite some time before they were in leadership. The sick are also excused. All others take their turn.

It is a weekly rotation so that everyone takes part over time. Especially at the beginning, it is important that each monk learn something about how the monastery functions. They learn from the bottom up and from the inside out. Those who come with high-minded ideas about study or contemplative life soon come face-to-face with the realities of running a monastery. We must all learn this.

The servers receive some extra bread and wine before serving the others during the meal. That way they will have plenty of strength. They eat their full meal afterward. It might also be viewed as one of the perks of the job that made many members more willing to do it! It keeps them less prone to grumble or complain while doing so.

On Saturday before the end of their weekly service, they wash the utensils and towels they used so that the incoming servers will have clean ones. This keeps us grounded in charity for others who must also have the tools to serve in charity. Then they hand them back to the cellarer, who keeps a list of all that is used. That way nothing is damaged, lost, or perhaps even stolen.

The outgoing and incoming servers are solemnly prayed over in church on Sunday to highlight the importance of the duty. Even manual labor is sacramentalized in the monastery, and no duty is beneath the divine origin of work.

Most monasteries today don't do this precisely or identically, but we all have our own version of it. In our integrated monastery we always start new members in manual labor and slowly teach them the various roles in community. We have a head cook and others help out. We pray over only the outgoing and incoming weekly prayer leaders, but we pray for our cooks, servers, and all who brought us our food at most every meal.

Meals are an important part of family and monastic community life. The Rule makes solemn the role of the cooks and servers. Each meal reminds us of the Eucharist and is sacramental. It is one of the blessings Benedict brings us today.

## Chapter 36

# The Sick Brothers

Care for the sick ranks above most everything else in the monastery. Jesus healed the sick as one of the main signs of his ministry. He bore our sicknesses and carried our sorrows on the cross. Because of this, his words had power for all time. Sometimes we try to preach before we act, and our words are empty. Benedict places care of the sick as a most high priority in the monastery. Then the other actions and words of the monks have real spiritual credibility and power.

The Rule grants the sick substantial concessions from normal monastic discipline and lifestyle. They have their own room apart from the common dormitory. Instead of serving, they are served by special attendants. They may take baths more often than the rest of the community. They do not fast but can eat red meat, something no one else can do. These are all serious concessions in the monastic discipline of the day. They are done for the love of God.

But the sick are not to take advantage of these concessions presumptuously. They are not to be demanding or cause undo distress for the community. They bear their sickness as a special gift of God to draw them and others closer through Christ. They remember that they are being especially served out of love for God and not due to their personal superiority. But even when they are demanding or complaining, we serve them patiently and with compassion. It is a sacrifice that fulfills us in return because we learn how to love more. That is our greatest reward.

Benedictine monasteries have been places of love and mercy for the poor and the sick throughout history. Before there were medical orders, missions, and hospitals, monasteries were caring for the sick monks and those who came to their door for special care. All later monastic traditions do the same. Eventually entire monastic communities that cared for the sick specialized in this tradition.

In our own time we have witnessed Mother Teresa of Calcutta who taught us that those who care for the sick and dying serve Jesus in a special way. We see the face of Christ even in the face of a faithless sick person. By seeing him there, we draw that person to the Christ they bear in their sickness. Today we face cancer, AIDS, and epidemics among those who have no means for medical care, not only in the developing world, but also in developed nations. Jesus says that when we care for the sick, we care for him. It all comes back to seeing Jesus in everyone. The sick are a special means of that grace. They teach us how to love.

Benedict foreshadows all these later traditions by building on the example of Jesus himself. He gives us a great blessing by implying that monasteries are not places for the superhuman but for the most human. He shows us how to make concessions for the weaknesses of others so that all might be healed. Monasteries are places of humble self-sacrifice and love. The greatest self-sacrifice is in loving the weak, the poor, and the sick. That is a most special blessing. Jesus and Benedict show us the way.

## Chapter 37

# The Elderly and Children

Monasteries are places where people live until death. That means that they grow old here. It is also a place where children are accepted. This is especially true with the new integrated monasteries of the new monastics. Children are born here and the elderly die here. We see the full spectrum of life in an integrated monastery.

There is a natural human compassion for the young and the old. In the young we see all the beautiful potential and innocence that adults might have lost at least to some degree. We love the elderly because they have given us all that is good in our physical, spiritual, and cultural life. They are grandfathers and grandmothers, great-aunts and -uncles. All the wisdom and memories of families and culture has been handed down through them. All these things are also true in a monastery as a spiritual family. If anything they are more pronounced because of the spiritual focus.

Monasteries are rather famous for their care of their elder monks. They are treated as wise grandparents, and they give the younger monks a tender care that only time can teach. Great spiritual transformations happen with the elderly. Even when their illness turns physically or emotionally tragic or embarrassing, we remember what they have given to us in their stronger years and that we will also be old someday. We treat others as we would like to be treated. It all comes back around.

The children in our integrated monastery also have sacred significance. Though ordinary in every respect, they are the Christ-child to the monastics. They keep us from getting too hard-hearted with them or with each other. How can you carry contempt for a monk who treats children kindly? This extended family is a joy to behold in a world where modern families are breaking down and are so dysfunctional. It is a sign of great hope.

Benedict says the elderly and children are not expected to live the full measure of the Rule. Concessions are made. They are weaker physically, emotionally, and intellectually. He specifically mentions food. We have already heard that the sick can eat meat. The elderly spend time in the infirmary, but this indicates something more general. Children are included in this provision. In our monastery we allow children, the elderly, and those with special medical needs more frequent and plentiful food, though they fast with us at the common table when bread or rice and beans and water are served as the main meal as a symbol of special times of self-sacrifice and control. Otherwise, we give them special treats to brighten their days with joy and encouragement.

The mention of food takes us back to the original treatment of kitchen servers and leads us to our next chapter regarding readers during meals. This loosely woven patchwork of topics indicates that the Rule probably developed over time. Chapters were likely written as circumstances arose, and they were inserted into a developing text. So let's return to the more natural flow of topics with readers. It is all a blessing of St. Benedict.

## Chapter 38

# The Weekly Readers

In modern culture we often gobble fast food way too fast! Even in religious houses we often scarf down processed food on the way to prayer or ministry. It is not healthy. It leads to overeating and obesity, bad digestion, and eventually to bad health. The Rule has a tool that helps overcome this modern destructive pattern.

The Rule of St. Benedict uses spiritual reading during meals. We listen in silence. This helps us to become reflective during meals, to slow down, eat less, and enjoy it more. It is healthier both spiritually and physically.

The readers rotate on a weekly basis. Everyone does not perform this ministry but only the ones who are truly able. We all have ministries, but we do not all have all ministries. The Spirit gives to each for the common good.

To emphasize the sacred character of this ministry, Benedict explains that the abbot and community bless the reader every Sunday after Mass and Communion in church. This also accentuates the parallel between the church and the refectory, or monastic dining room. Jesus is the Bread of Life. He is our life-giving spiritual food and drink and the Creator of the universe from which we gather earthly food and drink.

The ministry of reading is a service. Service involves sacrifice. The reader cannot eat with the community while reading so must wait until afterward. The reader eats with the other kitchen servers after the meal, but so that they will not grow weak, especially during fasts, they are given some diluted wine before they read.

We do not talk or whisper during the reading. That causes distraction and defeats its purpose. We may use signs to ask for utensils or food, but this can also distract so is kept to a minimum. We do not question the reading while it is being read. That would disrupt our meditation. The abbot may, however, add a brief word after the reading to apply it to the local community or make clarifications.

Today we emphasize mindful eating. We slow down, chew our food well, and thank God and those who helped bring it to the table as we eat. It is a culinary practice of meditation and gratitude that places us in communion with all creation and the Creator.

In our integrated monastery we use both reading and wholesome conversation at meals. Most modern monasteries in the West are similar. Our community begins with a reading from our Scripture Rule and Constitutions before the opening prayer and continues after the prayer with a spiritual book during the first ten minutes or so. After that we may recreate and speak freely. The reading tends to focus us on spiritual things so that we speak in a more positive way and do not degenerate into idle talk or gossip. This creates a spiritual and material family environment at meals. It remains an experience of healthy meditation, gratitude, and sharing. It is one of the blessings of the Rule that can be used in families or in monastic communities today.

Chapter 39

# The Proper Amount of Food

Now we come to the actual meal of the monks. The spiritual part of the meal is mentioned with reading first, then the physical content and amount of food. The spiritual precedes the physical, and the physical is not ignored, but it is spiritualized and made sacramental.

We live in a society that is suffering from an epidemic of gross obesity. Sixty percent of Americans are grossly overweight. We eat way too much and far too often. The early monks viewed gluttony as the first of eight vices. The Rule has an answer.

The Rule limits what a monk eats. But it is good food. There are only two meals a day, and ordinarily only one meal has two cooked dishes. Two dishes are provided in case a monk can eat only one, so he has a choice. When fruit or vegetables are available, they provide a third dish. The monks also receive a large portion of hearty, wholegrain bread for the entire day. It is ample fare.

The abbot can also add more food during times of extra labor and extreme climate. Children do not need as much as adults. Moderation is the rule, but even then, the main principle of monastic discipline is the overriding ideal. The gluttonous monk is alien to the tradition, and overindulgence is alien to Christianity.

Monks may eat meat but not of four-footed animals. Essentially this means white meat from fowl and fish but not red meat from livestock or game. Only the sick eat red meat during convalescence or recovery.

Most monasteries today offer the usual American fare, including red meat. Some limit themselves to white meat, and the Cistercians, Camaldolese, and non-Benedictine Carthusians are vegetarians, though they have made an art of it, so you do not miss meat at all! Almost all communities are facing the reality of obesity and related health issues and are actively promoting diet and exercise.

At Little Portion Hermitage we eat three meals a day, with one main community meal at noon. Our main meat is chicken from our free-range poultry farm, which also supplies eggs. We do eat red meat when it is given to us or from our organic farm. We grow most of our own vegetables from natural gardens. It is very healthy. We are also on a campaign to eradicate obesity from our members. We do not recommend going back for seconds unless it is necessary. We resist the comfort food reflex that hides our inability to deal with outer issues interiorly in Christ. We are far from perfect.

The answer is to eat well but not until one is completely satiated. Eating slowly and mindfully also gives the body time to gauge and stop before becoming overly full. In short, we eat to live but do not live to eat. We enjoy good food but are not addicted to it. Benedict points us in the right direction with these things with an ancient blessing from his Rule for monasteries. It still works well when adapted to modern life.

Chapter 40

# The Proper Amount of Drink

The Rule separates food and drink into two chapters, but there are really two related but distinct lessons for us here. The chapter on drink begins by saying that dictating the amounts of food and drink for another should be done hesitantly. We are not about controlling other people in God's name. We are about helping them with godly guidelines that work.

The ancient monastic tradition did not allow for monks to drink wine at all, but the Rule makes a concession for the monks of Benedict's day in order to bring them closer to that ancient ideal. Benedict allows for a moderate amount of wine, the normal daily drink of the folks at that time, but he does not tolerate drunkenness.

He also provides for abbots and monasteries that decide to provide less wine or none at all. He allows but does not dictate. This is done in relation to local circumstances, but he cautions against being too strict or stingy and causing the monks to grumble. This is to be avoided by the abbot meeting everyone's legitimate needs and through ready obedience on the part of the monks to their abbot.

Most monasteries today serve wine occasionally. I have rarely seen it as a standard part of the main monastic meals in America. Europe is different because wine is a more normal daily drink for everyone. But some in America and Europe bring out wine and hard liquor for special social events. Some communities specialize in producing fine liqueurs. None, however, condone drunkenness, though it must be admitted that alcoholism has shown up in monasteries as in many faith traditions.

At Little Portion we do not serve alcohol at meals. We only serve beer and wine on rare occasions when it is donated, and none are made to feel that they must drink. Hard liquor is never served. Nevertheless, we still have encountered members with substance abuse and addiction, including alcohol. If someone really wants it, they will get it whether or not we serve it at meals. We have been fortunate and have generally but not always been able to provide effective and affordable treatment that worked for the addicted members. For some people who struggle with these addictions, continuing in monastic life is ill-advised.

While the Rule addresses wine, we could easily expand this to sodas, coffee, and other caffeinated and sugar-laced drinks. These are often just as harmful and just as addictive. The ancient drink of choice by monks is pure water. At Little Portion we usually drink water at our main meals. We offer coffee in the kitchen for breakfast but caution against too much of it. We also provide sodas at special celebrations.

Benedict avoids addiction and overindulgence but is humane. He offers a way that is sacrificial but moderate, spiritual but physically sound, based on gospel ideals but practical enough for the average person wanting to follow the monastic way. And it works for us all. It is one of the blessings we find for daily life in the Rule.

Chapter 41

# The Times for Meals

Related to amount of food and drink is the time for meals. It teaches us to maintain a daily schedule and not just eat whenever the impulses of the flesh drive us, but it does satisfy genuine hunger. Though the schedule in the Rule seems very different from modern mealtimes, it also has lessons for us today.

The first meal is at noon during the celebratory seasons of Easter and Christmas. In Ordinary Time a midafternoon meal is taken around three. During Lent the meal is even later toward evening but not after dark so the meal could be eaten in daylight. The Rule does not mention another meal, but the Rule of the Master, which predates the Rule of Benedict by a few decades, mentions a second meal at supper of uncooked dishes. Benedict probably allowed this.

The entire monastic schedule rotated around the rising and setting of the sun, so times are measured not by a modern clock but rather by the hour after sunrise. That time was different in the summer and winter.

This schedule, called "fasting," means eating later and less. They ate daily, but it was seriously disciplined. Monks slept for eight hours after sundown. They arose around two or three o'clock in the morning for Vigils. On feast days after prayers and morning work they gathered for their noon meal. They ate another small meal toward evening, so it was a full eighteen hours or so before they would eat again. During "fast" days they waited until two or three o'clock in the afternoon, so it was nearly twenty hours between meals. During Lent they waited until late afternoon toward evening, so it was twenty-two or twenty-three hours before they ate. While not a full twenty-four hours between meals, this is still significant. Most modern monks I know simply couldn't do it.

John Cassian said that gluttony consisted of longing for food and drink when not really hungry and eating when not necessary between meals. The cure was fasting. He recommended not extreme fasting for entire days without meals but rather a constant and steady daily fast of reduced eating and drinking. Moderating earlier monastic traditions, the Rule of Benedict achieves that balance.

Most modern monasteries have three square meals a day, but they recommend moderate eating. At Little Portion we also have one main meal daily at noon for the entire community. Breakfast and supper are pick-up meals on your own for singles and celibates. Families eat breakfast and supper in their own domiciles. We do not recommend eating between meals except for a cold or hot drink break or a snack for those with extra work, medical needs, and for children and the elderly who need a bit more.

Benedict moderates the extreme fasts of early monasticism into a daily and livable whole. We do the same. Though we adapt it, the principle still works in monasteries or families today. It is one of the blessings of St. Benedict.

Chapter 42

## Silence after Compline

Silence for the sake of godly speech is maintained throughout the monastery at all times, but there are special times and places of silence as well. One of the traditional times is after the last Office of the day, Compline, or Night Prayer. It is often called the Great or Grand Silence.

This chapter also reveals a hidden treasure about a communal reading and reflection on the *Lives* and *Conferences* of the fathers or any other sacred book of tradition before Compline. The only exclusion is the first seven books of the Old Testament and the books of Kings, which are excluded presumably due to the violence contained in them. The Rule says that these are not good to hear right before bedtime but should be read at other times. This brings out the biblical, patristic, and ancient roots of monasticism and the importance of communal *lectio* and meditation. We must learn to meditate together as well as alone. It unites us on a deep spiritual level.

This communal reflection is done after supper (not specifically mentioned in chap. 27) in the church before Compline. It is meant to gather the members physically and mentally before the last prayer of the day. After Compline complete silence gracefully settles into the entire monastery.

This Great Silence is a special grace. Even the usual silence is quieted as the rustling of footsteps and the sound of opening and closing doors throughout the house gently comes to a standstill. All is settled, quiet, and calm.

This was especially needed in the early monastic communities where the members all slept in a common dormitory in a monastery that was under one roof. Everyone in that setting could hear even the smallest sounds of quiet speech and movement. The Great Silence gives everyone the grace of peace and quiet for prayer and sleep.

Today most monasteries have dormitories with private rooms. Even in this setting the Great Silence is a gift. Hermitages do not need this practice as much since the silence of solitude is automatic, but even there it is helpful where hermitages are within earshot of one another. The Grand Silence is a great gift to all.

We even recommend times and places for silence with monastic families and domestics who live in their own homes. Some say it cannot be done with children, but our experience is that children take to silence very beautifully when it is presented well. When made a "special" time to be with Jesus, children find great fun and mystery in it. Plus, if the parents or adults are at peace themselves, then they can pass that spirit on to children. If they are agitated within, then they can only pass on agitation. If we are agitated by agitation itself, it only makes the agitation worse. It is a great gauge for one's inner condition. Outer silence comes from and aids inner silence and peace. Children perceive these things intuitively.

In our noisy modern world, the silence of this ancient Rule is a blessing to us all.

## Chapter 43

**Tardiness**

There is an old saying, "If you want to get something done, give it to a busy person." They are busy precisely because they are good. They are good because they are considerate and punctual in their work and life. The same is true in monasteries.

There are some who are always busy but never get much of anything done well. They are habitually tardy to everything and negligently late in what they do. They have less to do because they cannot be trusted with the little they have to do and yet are still late to everything. The Rule addresses this sad syndrome.

Benedict's monasteries have a definite daily schedule for life. This is meant as a corrective for those who have little or no personal discipline, but sometimes even that does not work. The Rule sets down consequences to give further help to the individual and the community.

This chapter mainly mentions lateness to prayer or community meals. A signal is used to call the community together, and we are to lay aside whatever we are doing privately for the greater community good. It allows for some to come late up to a point. After that point they undergo discipline. That usually meant not sitting in your normal place in the church but taking the lowest seat or having to eat after the community was finished. These are practical measures. It minimizes disruption to the prayer service or meal. It is also an object lesson to the tardy and the community.

This chapter also addresses not eating between meals. We do not eat before the appointed time. As noted before, John Cassian said that this is a sign of gluttony. Additionally, this chapter mentions vacillation in receiving something extra from the abbot. We either take it or we don't. People who cannot make up their minds about such little things as receiving extra food will probably have problems with greater things.

Modern monasteries also face the problem of tardiness. In a secular workplace a habitually late person simply loses his or her job. Monasteries tend not to take those so inclined, but we do take some. We also use appropriate measures to correct this syndrome. We usually ask those who come to work late to stay later to make up what they neglected. At Little Portion we also use a weekly chapter meeting where everyone confesses their failings and are prayed over for strength and forgiveness.

Tardiness, procrastination, or unnecessary absence are ultimately expressions of selfishness. It means that we place ourselves over the community functions that others must attend. If we all came only when we liked, nothing would work well in a monastery. It is not an individual experience. It is communal. It teaches us to sacrifice self for the sake of God and others. In so doing we find ourselves made new into a better person. Some are conditioned for tardiness by their upbringing and past cultural experiences. The Rule is a way to heal that defect. It is a blessing from God through St. Benedict.

## Chapter 44

# Satisfaction and Forgiveness

We have already generally addressed the topic of this chapter with excommunication for faults (chap. 23). But it deserves a brief elaboration. It has a lesson to teach on its own and can bless us still today.

Those who make various mistakes are corrected as an aid in their spiritual progress. After continued habitual mistakes and several warnings they are given specific aids called penances. These are usually public in nature. The element of a public object lesson is not absent, but it is not the only element. Its real goal is to heal, not to punish or shame, and even less to control. God alone is the Lord. But these measures are real and they are sometimes tough.

Those who make truly serious mistakes are to prostrate themselves before the abbot and the feet of all. This is done at the end of the Work of God at the entrance of the church. This sounds extreme to modern ears but was an accepted penance in the early church for public sinners seeking the forgiveness of all. Then the abbot calls the monk to prostrate themselves again in church so that the entire community might pray for them. Likewise, the offending monk prays the Office in prostration before God and the community. This is radical, but the goal is prayer and conversion, not punishment.

If the penitent monk perseveres without anger or resentment, it is a sign that they are ready to change. Then the abbot can call an end to the process with the assurance that the monk has changed in heart and action. For less serious faults a similar but less intense process is used. When all this has been done the abbot can say, "Enough." From that point on, it is over and done with. Forgiveness is offered publically, and the community puts it behind them.

Scripture says that Jesus forgives every sin if we but turn back to him with all our heart, but we are not to presume forgiveness without a genuine change of heart. That is why John the Baptizer calls religious people to bring forth "fruits worthy of repentance." There must be a tangible sign of change or it is all a sham. The early church instituted this liturgically with public penance for serious publically known crimes. The monastic community continued it in their own setting.

We also find modern ways for this process to unfold in community. Matters that touch the community are addressed in a community meeting, or chapter. This is communal, though meetings are strictly internal family matters and not shared outside the community. Confession there is communal, as is the forgiveness offered. The end result is not unhealthy manipulation or control of members' lives by others but a communal support that helps us all to change. Matters that do not affect the community in the public forum are left to private processes with a sacramental confessor or spiritual director. But the community exists as a support in our mutual process of conversion in Christ.

The Rule offers a pattern that worked well sixteen hundred years ago. The general principles still work well today when appropriately used. It is one of the blessings of Benedict.

Chapter 45

# Mistakes in Church

Most people of my generation remember a time when correct behavior in church was simply expected as the norm, but sometimes instead of making us feel like we were in the house of a loving God, it made us feel like we were in the house of a litigious, demanding, and angry Lord. It was a bit obsessive. We have tried to reverse that with greater comfort before Jesus in church. But we have also seen it lapse into a negligence that does not befit the house of God. The Rule of Benedict can help us rediscover the balance between these two extremes.

The Rule says that we must try not to make mistakes in church. That would primarily mean during the Work of God, the Divine Office. It also means during Communion or Mass. If we do make mistakes, though, we do not just act like nothing happened. We simply acknowledge it and move forward.

Benedict does not specify how that humble acknowledgment took place. Judging from the rest of the Rule it probably meant something like a bow. Historically, a monk would briefly kneel or prostrate himself if there was room and then keep going. In those days it was not a real big deal.

But failure to acknowledge the mistake was. It indicated a presumption and negligent attitude that could be problematic in spiritual and practical, private and communal life. In that case a more severe penance occurred, probably more like what we see in other places in the Rule. The principle of proportion is seen throughout the Rule.

Children were given corporal punishment. This was because they did not understand the more subtle aspects of such things yet but could understand consequences. This was not as punitive as it sounds to modern ears.

Today we generally do not use these means or measures. Monastics specialize in liturgies that are beautiful but peaceful. Most of us want the liturgy to be good. If we fail at points, we ask pardon of God interiorly and move on. If it is very public and affects the general worshiping community by a mistake in reading or leading, we might appropriately pause briefly and ask pardon. Then we proceed. Making too much of it can actually make the worship experience worse. The point is to have a good liturgy and for all to come closer to God through community prayer.

In our integrated monastery children also participate at some but not all Offices and at Mass. They are readers once a week and altar servers. They dress in a modified version of our habit, are neatly groomed, and are generally alert and attentive. They usually do a great job. When they do not, they are corrected. When they are habitually negligent, they do not get to participate in the special ministry until they are ready to change. That is usually quite enough to keep things straight. They are a joy at liturgy.

Though seemingly extreme by modern standards, the Rule provides an ancient basis for healthy modern guidelines in public prayer. It is a blessing from St. Benedict.

## Chapter 46

# Faults in Other Matters

The Rule mainly addresses major faults in church or at table, but there are many other areas in a monastery where success and failure occur. Monasteries are extraordinary places built on the events of ordinary daily life. There are all manner of workplaces in a functioning monastery. The Rule mainly mentions the kitchen, storeroom, the bakery, garden, and craft areas. In addition to these, there were other places and jobs.

We have already heard that we are to treat the tools of the monastery like the sacred vessels of the altar, but sometimes we break things accidentally or lose them. Or sometimes we do a job that is not as good as what is expected by others or ourselves.

When this occurs we are to go at once and confess it to the abbot and the community. We are not to be afraid but trust that any actions will help us in the future. Sometimes this is tougher and more embarrassing than we would like. Scripture says that such disciplines seem hard, but they are for our greater good and are offered in love, so we should submit ourselves to them unless they are clearly and habitually abusive.

But sometimes we hide our mistakes, and leaders become aware of the mistake through the report of others.

This is sad and creates a communication breakdown that is dangerous to any good business or monastery. When that happens greater measures are used. It is no longer a small matter but something more serious.

When this happens the one who has made the mistake reveals this darkness hidden in their conscience to the abbot or one of the delegated spiritual fathers in private. In monastic tradition this is called monastic confession or revelation of thoughts. This is distinct from sacramental confession of actual sins. This is an ancient, voluntary practice between a monk and his spiritual father. The spiritual father helps the monk to be healed and for light to shine freely in their soul, but they keep the confession private. This is most significant in a Rule where so much correction occurs publically. It displays understanding and a gentle care that is Christlike.

In our community we often use a similar process when members fail in daily work. Perhaps because of past experiences of secular life they try to hide their failure from the community. But everyone knows that someone did it, and perhaps they even know who it was. You can keep very little secret in monastic community. The best cure is a public apology in community chapter, where all such things are confidential to the community alone. Usually the mistake or loss has affected other people. The community appreciates the honesty. If a public apology is not going to happen, then a private confession to the monastic father is sufficient. The confessor usually recommends going to those involved and asking forgiveness as well, and it is almost always given.

This process of responsibility and forgiveness is one of the blessings of Benedict.

Chapter 47

# Announcing the Work of God

A monastery is a body, so the members move in a coordinated manner; otherwise, we are disjointed and ineffective. This coordination requires some planning and effort. This brief chapter on the signal for prayers brings that principle to light.

A signal is sounded before common prayers to alert the monks so that they can close up shop and join together in the church. They cannot just come when they feel like it, or there would be no common prayer services. And they cannot come at leisure, or people will be walking in throughout the service, disrupt the focus, and distract the community from meaningful prayer. Anarchy does not motivate monks.

The abbot makes sure that the signal is sounded. It is ultimately his responsibility since prayer is the most important communal work in the monastery, but he may delegate it to another monk who he trusts to be responsible in the ministry. This illustrates the larger principle of coordination of life under obedience to the abbot throughout the monastery. It also is a communal aid for the individual monks to keep a disciplined daily schedule. Without it some monks would fritter their lives away in false contemplation.

In most Western monasteries this is normally done with a bell. It is rung anywhere from fifteen to five minutes before the Office. We ring a bell at fifteen and five minutes before prayers so that monastics can begin putting things away at fifteen till and actually enter the church around five till. Some who work out on the farm or in workshops also make use of watch alarms. We do not recommend coming in later than five minutes before prayer. This gives each one time to settle in and quiet their hearts and minds before we actually start the Office. Otherwise, prayers take on an anxious and scattered tone.

This chapter also brings out the principles of service and obedience. Only those authorized to do so may lead the chants of the psalms and canticles or proclaim the Scripture or fathers. Only those who really have a God-given gift engage in this important ministry. The abbot is first in ministering these things, and others do so with the abbot's permission. This ensures a proper humility in ministry itself. We do not claim a ministry for our own. It is God's, and the community and the abbot discern its genuineness. Otherwise, it may just be ego under the guise of charism.

In our community we have a weekly prayer leader from the professed monastics. It is an honor to lead prayer, not a right, but we try to rotate through as many as feel called to lead and have the gift to do so. Perfection is not required. Cantors lead the singing and help keep us on track musically. Readers sign up similarly, but only those who proclaim well usually want or are allowed to do so. Most realize when it is not their gift.

It is good to have a prayer schedule that is bigger than our own whims. It is good to submit our will to an external call from community and leaders. It is also good to recognize our gift and use it humbly in community. This is a blessing of St. Benedict.

Chapter 48

# Manual Labor and Reading

We are spiritual and physical beings. We have sensual bodies and spiritual souls. The Rule addresses each with work and sacred reading. This chapter specifically mentions labor and reading. This opens the way for the contemplation of the spirit. This fully integrates our human being as spirit, soul, and body in the divine.

The chapter begins with an ancient monastic quote that "idleness is the enemy of the soul." The main title of the chapter is on manual labor, but within this chapter we find a rather full treatment on classical spiritual reading, or *lectio divina*.

If all we do is pray and read, we become mentally strained and obsessed. If all we do is work, we become physically exhausted and too tired to read or pray. We need a little of both to balance each. This chapter emphasizes that human need for balance. It is in this chapter that we find the famous Benedictine axiom, "all things are to be done with moderation" (see 48.9). We are to find a healthy middle ground between extremes.

Work was commended as the way of the ancient Desert Fathers who said that the entire life of the monk is manual labor. Though helpers were ordinarily hired for harvesting the fields, it remains the special privilege of the monks of St. Benedict.

The Rule allotted an average of around six hours a day to work and about three to *lectio*. *Lectio* was generally the first couple of hours in the morning after Office and before work. The monks also either rested or read after the Noon Office and meal. During Lent more time is given to *lectio*. Sundays were spent almost entirely in *lectio*. The sick and those who couldn't were given some simple work to do while praying.

Normally the content for *lectio* was Scripture. But during Lent the members were given other sacred books from the library to read straight through. A haphazard reading discipline was not practiced. Senior monks made the rounds to ensure that all were doing *lectio* and not engaging in idle talk that is harmful to the soul.

Today some monks say that the Rule provides a life that is half work and half prayer. Others say one-third work, one-third *lectio*, and one-third sleep. (This does not include time in community meetings and upkeep of the cell.) The Rule itself adapts the amount for each to the variation of the seasons, taking into account available light, liturgical practice, and personal sacrifice.

Most modern monasteries have adapted to a modern work schedule of a forty-hour workweek, or six to eight hours a day for five or six days. The genuine material and spiritual needs of the monastic community must be considered and balanced. At Little Portion we put in about a six- to eight-hour workday, depending on the needs of the farm and publishing ministry schedules. We adapt to the needs of the season.

We all need work and prayer, labor and *lectio*, and the moderation of both for a balanced spiritual life. It brings health and joy. It is one of the blessings of Benedict.

Chapter 49

# The Observance of Lent

Lent is the period leading up to Easter based on the forty-day fast of Jesus in the desert. It was observed from the early days of the church and still is today.

The Rule says that monastic life is a "perpetual Lent." In a sense, every liturgical season is lived every day during the natural unscheduled ups and downs of life. Still, even monastics observe liturgical Lent along with the rest of the church. This helps unite them with the church universal in focusing on that aspect of life in Christ.

We have already heard how the Rule codifies a moderate daily fast instead of more complete abstinence of special days. Yet, during Lent a little something extra is recommended. We pray and work a bit more and eat and sleep a bit less. We do a bit more than what we normally do, even though monastic life is already going the extra mile as a perpetual Lent for Jesus. But this is not drudgery. It is something we do with joy as we prepare ourselves for Easter and being raised up even more fully in Christ.

This is not a purely individual thing. We are part of a community, a cenobium, and we are under the spiritual direction of an abbot and his delegates. We submit all of our personal Lenten practices to the local abbot for his approval. This is not about manipulation or control. It is part of the "revelation of thoughts," or monastic confession, of the monk to the abbot or spiritual father. Many go to extremes in religious practice, and some do not go far enough, and this is meant to moderate such excesses for the well-being of the monk. The Rule requires this to keep us individually on track. This in turn helps keep the monastery spiritually and functionally on track as well.

At Little Portion we normally fast on bread and water or other similar food on Wednesdays and Fridays unless health or work require some moderation. During Lent we become more rigorous in tone. Lent is a more focused practice. It is a magnified microcosm of monastic sacrifice. We mainly ask that members examine their spiritual life and remove the things that can impede the Spirit from flowing freely. It is about becoming more like Jesus.

We ask that all our monastics submit a list of their Lenten practices to their respective leaders. This is especially valuable at the beginning of monastic life, since the new member is still getting the hang of it. With older members the leader rarely amends much of anything, but we have the option to do so if necessary. It moderates the religiously scrupulous, directs and focuses the scattered, and motivates the lethargic. It is a most helpful pastoral tool.

The Rule encourages everyone to take full advantage of Lent and to intentionally focus on going the extra mile in following Jesus in the monastic tradition. It also encourages submitting that practice to a spiritual father or mother to keep us from lapsing into spiritual individualism and pride. It is one of the blessings of St. Benedict.

Chapters 50–51

# Monks Working at a Distance or Traveling and on a Short Journey

Monks in the time of Benedict did not travel much. Ordinarily only the abbot and other leaders traveled for business or ministry. The average monk stayed within or close to the monastery all his life and rarely left the local area. The same was true of society in general. Travel was rare.

Modern monastics in the West live in a time where just about everyone travels hundreds or even thousands of miles from home every year for business or pleasure. Monastics do the same, albeit more for ministry. This can create external and internal instability that is not good for monastic life. The Rule codifies stability in obedience to an abbot as a cure for the gyrovague syndrome addressed in chapter 1 of the Rule. But it also allows for some travel. It provides a balance of stability and itinerancy. It is also helpful for serious Christians today.

The greatest aid for stability during travel is maintaining the prayers of the Work of God, or Liturgy of the Hours. When away from the monastery monks pray the Hours. They kneel where they are and pray some version of the Office. Most committed the Office to memory, which kept them in union with their monastery even when away from it. This also allowed them to share the blessings of the Hours with others.

But prayer does not keep the members from the other active ministries and works that take them away from the monastery in the first place. Just as in the monastery, prayer leads to ministry and ministry leads back to prayer. They form a rhythm that complements and completes one another. They become a prayer.

Those who go out for day trips do not linger but come back to the monastery as soon as possible and do not eat outside unnecessarily. This is hard when friends press monastics to join them. But the abbot can give permission for this when appropriate and helpful to the purpose.

Most modern monks travel. It is certainly part of our life at Little Portion. My ministry takes me out for long periods of time. Others do so on occasion, and most all take annual vacations. Day trips in the local area are necessary for the upkeep and prosperity of the monastery and our ministries.

When we travel outside the monastery we try to pray at least Morning and Evening Prayer. There are breviaries, or abbreviated versions of the Work of God, for both the monastic and diocesan church today that work very well. We may go to dinner with others but not normally as mere recreation. It all focuses on ministry to the monastery and others. We are not self-indulgent during travel.

When we travel we become a traveling monastery unto ourselves. We take the monastery with us wherever we go. That is how we spread the Gospel as monastics. It makes the entire world a monastery and all our life a prayer. It is one of the blessings of St. Benedict.

Chapter 52

# The Oratory of the Monastery

In today's highly secularized and noisy world people often feel a need for sacred space. These are places for meditation and prayer. These are places free of clutter and where simple sacred objects help to focus our faith. The Rule provides for the monastic oratory or church. It is the most sacred space in the monastery.

Monasteries can also be busy places. Contrary to popular belief, it is a place where ordinary monks do all the ordinary things of life with extraordinary faith, hope, and love. Typically there are kitchens, workshops, farm fields, and guesthouses, not to mention ministry offices and schools at various levels. A typical monastery bustles, albeit with silent and peaceful activity for God. If not, it is either dead or dying.

In the midst of that activity is the oratory, the place for *oratio*, prayer. It is the heart of the entire community. It is the still point in time and the calm in the midst of the storm. It calls us all to the most important activity any of us can do: pray. It is what makes all our activity divine. All activity flows from prayer and leads back to prayer.

The oratory is a place big enough for the entire community to gather. It is a monastic church. But it is only used for prayer. Ordinarily nothing else is done there. The greatest prayer is the community celebration of the Work of God and the Eucharist. We have heard that God is present everywhere but especially during the Work of God, which, along with the Eucharist, is the "source and summit" of monastic life.

But it is also used for private prayer. In Benedict's monasteries there was very little time or space to be alone. The "cell" where private sacred reading was done was one's bed area in a common dormitory. The solitary cell was the dwelling of the hermit. The oratory provided a place for the private prayer of the cenobitical monk.

The greatest characteristic of the oratory is silence. We are not silent during the Work of God, so this refers to the times for private prayer. We do not pray privately with a loud voice. This can distract from the prayer of others. Nevertheless, it is to be heartfelt, so we can pray with quiet and humble tears. Those who do not pray in this quiet way are not to stay in the oratory between services.

Today the monastic church is used for both public and private prayer. The cell is more private for most modern monks, so the majority of private prayer and *lectio* is done there. Still, the church works well for those who wish to come early or stay after the Office for prayer. Others find it convenient to make little visits there throughout the day while working in the monastery. At Little Portion we do the same. Praying in church throughout the day is better for those whose cells are a distance from the common center in our monastic village, especially in bad weather. The church is the warm, spiritual heart of the monastic community.

Most of us need sacred spaces today. It helps to balance the secular and profane we must face almost daily. It is a sacred blessing of St. Benedict.

Chapter 53

# The Reception of Guests

"Guests are never lacking in a monastery" (see 53.16). In peaceful times people of all states of life, religions, and ideologies come to visit these havens of prayer. As the soul is to the body and the chapel is to the monk, so the monastery is to the world. They are the often-unseen spiritual heart of humanity. Once folks awaken to that reality, they often want to visit monasteries. Benedict provides for them to "come and see."

The Rule says we receive all guests as we would Christ. It does not say "some," or the just the ones we like or those well thought of in the world. It says "all." Because of this, hospitality has become a special ministry of monasteries all around the world.

But there is a clear spiritual emphasis in the act of receiving guests. Monasteries are not hotels, museums, or tourist attractions, though pilgrims are always welcome. There is an elaborate quasi-liturgical reception provided for in the Rule. The entire community and superior meet the guest with prayer. Then comes the welcoming kiss of peace, a deep prostration before them as Christ among us, then more prayer, and meditation on some Scripture. After that an ordinary, kind welcome is shown with a meal with the abbot, who may break his fast on account of the guest. Even there, the abbot washes the hands and feet of the guest before the meal. Again we are reminded that it is Christ we receive in the guest.

Special guest rooms are also provided for. The abbot's table is set up especially for guests, with monks to wait on them. But when there are no guests these monks go back to other ordinary monastic duties. A guesthouse with a wise guest master is provided so that their needs may be taken care of responsibly. Sometimes guests can be a handful for the less experienced.

Besides these rather extraordinary measures, the monks are not to associate with guests. This may sound strange, but monks found that it was all too easy to be drawn into unnecessary conversation and gossip otherwise. They simply give a sacred greeting and briefly ask for a blessing when they meet a guest. They explain that they may not speak otherwise. This is often a great ministry of sacred silence.

Today most monasteries welcome guests as Christ but in a more relaxed and casual manner. They have separate guest facilities and guest masters. While abbots often visit with them, guests usually have their own dining room or a separate area in the monastic dining room. At Little Portion we have guest hermitages with a guest master. We also operate a separate retreat center with a staff away from the monastery. At the monastery guests eat with the community and sometimes join the head table with me. Some eat with the other members of the community.

Christians today need to rediscover the ministry to guests. They are the presence of Jesus to us under the appearance of the guest. The ministry of hospitality is a unique monastic gift to the world. It is a most special blessing of St. Benedict.

## Chapter 54

## Letters and Gifts for Monks

The monks of the Rule of St. Benedict live a strictly cenobitical, or communal, life. They do not keep any personal possessions but share all things in common after the example of Acts 2 and 4. This is a huge sacrifice.

But personal possessions creep back into monastic life when monastics begin keeping a little bit back for themselves. Little by little we can regain all the attachment we thought we had renounced when we entered the monastery. It can kill the spirit of a monastery if left unchecked. Benedict addresses this reality by forbidding monks to keep gifts, even ones from parents and friends.

It is rather amazing how those who give up substantial possessions and control of their own life in the world in order to enter a monastery will sometimes lose their zeal by getting bogged down by seemingly insignificant things once they have joined a community. It seems such a tragedy to lose the fire of one's monastic vocation over something that would have been next to nothing in the world, but it is not uncommon.

Monks may keep some things given by family or friends so long as they are first disclosed to the abbot. The abbot then decides how to disperse them. He almost never keeps them entirely from the individual monastic when they are received with Christian love for all the monks. But he may share a larger gift with everyone. Community life is based on love that shares freely with all.

Monasteries are not heartless places. Monastic life and renunciation better dispose us to love because we are now free from personal prejudice that comes from attachment. We actually become better family members by renouncing our past patterns of family based on ego, possession, and control. We are separated from all to be united with all. And we renounce all to gain everything.

Gifts from parents and friends are first given to community. Then the abbot may give what he discerns back to us. And we can freely enjoy them. The parent and family of one become the parent and family of all. We do not lose a family but gain a bigger one. We do not lose such gifts and tokens, but they find a bigger and better meaning in Christ. This little miracle of multiplication is always a joy to behold.

Today monks renounce personal inheritances but may usually keep small gifts from family and friends. This keeps a monastery loving, compassionate, and kind. If, however, there is a danger that the monk may become attached to the things that were once renounced, the monk is not to keep the gift. Larger gifts and donations are given to the community and then to the individual monastic. Most family and friends of monks understand this and give most big things for the entire community to enjoy.

The Rule reminds us not to lose our greater gifts by attaching to smaller ones. We give it all to God, then God gives us what we need, and we are free to enjoy it. In a culture attached to consumerism and control, this is a great blessing indeed.

Chapter 55

# The Clothing, Footwear, and Bedding of the Monks

Clothing is a very personal thing. It not only serves the function of protection from the elements but also expresses our personality. Nevertheless, many people are vain and consumeristic about clothing today. Monastics renounce their old patterns of using possessions, and even their very self, to be fully reborn in Christ. This includes their clothing. The Rule outlines the typical monk's clothing, often called a "habit."

We often picture monks in black or brown robes with hoods. Our images are often overly romantic. Something far more practical was the reality.

The Rule actually gives the abbot considerable leeway as to what the monks may wear. It recommends rather typical attire for people in temperate climates. Most folks wore a long tunic and a hood, or cowl, and an apron for work called a "scapular." The tunic was girded up during work. They could wear sandals or shoes, presumably in summer and winter, respectively. Later in history these things were given religious significance, but the Rule is silent about such symbolism. It is similar enough to the clothing of the day that it could be given to the poor but distinct enough to be called a monk's garb. It was simple, poor, and distinctive.

Monks were not to complain about the quality or color of their clothes. They were given thick habits for winter and thinner ones for summer. They were made of inexpensive cloth. The color usually varied based on the time of the year wool was obtained. It was darker in the winter and lighter in the summer. They had two habits so that one could be washed while wearing another.

The abbot was to ensure that their habits fit properly. He also gave those going on a journey something a little nicer than usual with special underclothes. But this was all relinquished after the journey. The daily clothing of the monks was common and simple. That is about all they personally possessed, and even these were considered community property. All belonged to Christ.

The only other personal things were the bed of the monk and a few small items. They received a mat, heavy and light blankets, and a pillow. By the standards of that time and place this was sufficient and ample. An inspection of beds and personal items was regularly conducted to make sure that monks were not holding anything back from the abbot or the community. But the abbot also made sure that legitimate needs were met so that there would be no excuse for hoarding and hiding personal possessions. Clothing and personal work and writing items are specifically mentioned.

Today monastics wear a habit and sleep in simple but comfortable beds in a private cell. The habit is distinct from lay clothing but simple enough to be worn inside the monastery for most tasks. Simple secular clothes are often used during manual labor. We properly care for personal clothes, grooming, and possessions, but we are not attached to them. We have renounced all. That is a blessing of monastic life that works for everyone in all states of life. It is a blessing of St. Benedict.

## Chapter 56

# The Abbot's Table

The abbot is the spiritual father of the community. He is a part of the family but holds a special place within it. He is a conduit of creative energy in the family. He is redeemed by Christ with all the others but holds the place of Christ as an instrument of redemption for all the others. This is reflected in the eating arrangements for the abbot in the Rule.

The Rule of Benedict provides a separate table, kitchen, and dining room for the abbot. The Rule of the Master, which preceded the Rule of Benedict, dictates that the abbot eats with the monks. But this separate dining room is not established out of disdain for the monks. It is actually a ministry to them.

The abbot normally eats with the guests of the monastery, and these can be an intrusion into the stability of the monks. Eating separately protects the monks from this intrusion, much like not having company at a family meal too often.

It is also a place where the abbot can dine with individual monks and give them special attention. This is an honor for the monks and an opportunity for ministry by the abbot. It is a time for special bonding by sharing a meal together and talking about the things of God one-on-one.

But the monks' dining room is not left unsupervised. Seniors eat with the monks to provide oversight and discipline as prescribed by the Rule for table procedures. That ensures both an orderly spiritual and physical repast in Christ.

Today most abbots eat at a head table in a common dining room with the monks. Guests either eat in a guest dining room regularly visited by the abbot or in the monastic dining room at a special place. A separate dining room for abbots is still maintained by some and used on special occasions.

At Little Portion we have a head table for the spiritual father and mother. Guests are often seated there and community members rotate to share a meal with us there. On the rare occasion of special guests we may eat with them privately.

Abbots and other monastery officials are part of the daily discipline of a monastery but are often called away for ministry and leadership responsibilities. This is seen both with prayer and meals. Communities understand this dynamic, but abbots are not exempt from the monastic life in general, and too much absence from community activities erodes their authority to speak to the community.

This seemingly insignificant chapter is really rich with lessons about these familial and communal dynamics. In a monastery, ordinary things take on spiritual significance that are rich with spiritual and practical symbolism. It is not to be passed over lightly but meditated on, pondered, and practiced. It is one of the blessings of the Rule for our time.

## Chapter 57

## The Artisans of the Monastery

Monasteries are rather ordinary places. They are where heaven comes to earth in the ordinary things of daily life. They are a spiritual village of sorts where most of the normal things of life in a little town also occur. Work is a biblical obligation and a great honor and privilege. It is also a monastic virtue. Monks are given work so they might pray better. We pray and work, *ora et labora*. The Rule acknowledges and provides for this.

Monks are people with ordinary needs for food, clothing, and shelter. They work for a living like everyone else. This means that goods are produced and sold in and from the monastery. Monastics are also creative human beings who use their gifts for God, the church, and humanity.

The Rule provides guidelines for the artisans of the monastery. Monks are free to use their God-given talents to produce crafts within the monastery itself. A monastery is filled with workshops of every kind and offices to administrate their sale to the world. This ministers to the world through the quality work of the monks and provides an income to the monks, who are to be self-supportive by the work of their hands.

But monks are not to become proud or possessive of their talents and work. If it becomes a source for these vices, it is to be prohibited until the monk can rediscover his humility and detachment. Only then is the monk or his work really free. Monks are given what they need to do their work, but they do not possess either the workspaces or the instruments of their craft. It all belongs to God and is insured by common ownership in the monastery.

To ensure this humility and detachment, the articles the artists produce are to be sold at a somewhat lower price than those of the world. Our work should be more careful, and our prices more charitable. We offer the world more for less in order to win most of the world for God. But it is not given away either, except for special ministry to the poor. That would cheapen its value in the minds of the secular world. It must also be admitted that this is a very shrewd business tool!

Monasteries are famous for the production of finely crafted things. These range from food and farms to books and beer to music and ministry. Monastics specialize in the overtly sacred and mundane and making all things sacred through prayer. They have done it all. And they have done all things well.

At Little Portion we do much the same. We produce music and books, religious arts and crafts, free-range poultry, organic vegetables and beef, and operate a retreat center. We must also maintain a monastery to house and feed over thirty people daily. This is all hard work. But it is also a great joy and privilege, especially in a time when so many are without wholesome work. It is one of the blessings from the Rule of St. Benedict for all who work for a living every day.

Chapter 58

# The Procedure for Receiving New Brothers

Many are attracted to monastic spirituality. There's a bit of a monk in every seeker. Some actually try the life, but not everyone is really called to it by God. Some make it, and some do not. Many are called and few are chosen. To expect everyone to stay is unrealistic. To expect no one to do so is a self-fulfilling prophecy that will kill the morale of those who stay. The Rule presents a way of testing the call of those who try and of ordinarily expecting a lifetime commitment for those who stay.

In the Rule, the test begins at the monastery door. Candidates were to wait four or five days before being allowed to enter. The principle was to see if they were really serious before even letting them try, but they did not enter fully yet. First they stayed in the guesthouse for a few days. Only after that were they allowed to enter the monastery as new members, or novices.

The novitiate is the place and time for novices. It is a one-year time of testing while entering slowly into the full life of the monastic community. Novices and community are mutually discerned. The Rule is studied and lived. An elder monk oversees the progress. A novice may leave after two, eight, or twelve months. After that the novice is received into full membership.

He is received before the entire community and abbot in the church. He promises stability, faithfulness to monastic life (conversion of life), and obedience before all and in the presence of God and the saints. This is solemnly confirmed by a legal document in the name of the saint whose relics are present and the abbot. It is written in his own hand if he can write and placed personally and voluntarily on the altar. He prostrates himself before each monk, who prays for the new member.

At this time the new monk divests himself of all possessions. He may give them to the monastery if he wishes but may not keep anything for himself. He is stripped of his clothing and garbed in the monastic habit as a sign of his personal poverty, but the monastery keeps his secular clothes to give back in case, God forbid, the monk leaves or is dismissed. The monastery keeps the document in perpetuity.

Today candidates go through a modern screening process involving visits, pastoral interviews, and psychological screening. The novitiate is one to two years during which the new member studies specific monastic spirituality and history and lives the monastic life. They usually stay in a separate part of the monastery but pray, eat, and work with the other monks. Sometimes they receive a partial form of the habit and only receive the full habit upon profession. Today they make an additional temporary profession of the vows that can last from three to nine years. After that a monk is received into permanent profession. If they depart or are dismissed, charity is shown and reasonable aid is given to help them reenter secular life.

Today many seek monastic spirituality. Some enter monasteries, and some live an inner monasticism in the world.

The Rule blesses us all with a discernment process for what form that calling will take. It is a blessing of St. Benedict.

## Chapter 59

# The Offering of Sons by Nobles or by the Poor

Children are a great blessing to the church and the world. They are also a blessing for monasteries. Children were received in ancient monasteries. They were "offered" as an "oblation" by both the wealthy and the poor. This is the foundation of what would become the oblates of modern monasteries.

In those times the firstborn were granted the lion's share of the inheritance of the wealthy family. The second child was to assist the firstborn. The later-born children had a diminished role in the family estate. These children were often donated to monasteries. There they were given the finest education of the day and a quality life. Boys usually became clerics. Poor families did something similar. It was a way to give a child a life with stability, although in a lesser station than those of the wellborn. But even these could go on to become leaders in the monastery and the church. This was not a bad deal at all for the children. And the monasteries got a steady stream of vocations from the children donated to them by faithful families.

This arrangement developed through the years. Monasteries began operating schools at every level. Some of these were residential boarding schools, and some were higher education to train young people for service in both the secular world and the church. From these many vocations were fostered for those who wanted to become monks or sisters.

The rise of the Third Orders for those who lived in the secular world but associated with the spirituality and lifestyle of the mendicants like the Franciscans and Dominicans also affected monasteries. The oblate program, originally for children, was adapted for adults who associated with monasteries and lived monastic spirituality in the secular world. This also included "residential oblates" for those who could not give up all their possessions but who lived in the monastery as valued participants in every other way.

At our integrated monastery at Little Portion we include singles and families with children. These keep more private property than the celibate monks and sisters, but are a most valuable part of the community. Children are a great blessing to the integrated monastery. They keep celibates childlike in their faith and receive a daily extended family that has long since disintegrated in Western culture where families are so spread out. Of course, we use all the necessary safeguards to protect them from abuse by adults.

As in the ancient times, this arrangement assists families seeking better faith environments in which to raise a family and foster new vocations of every kind for the monastery and the church. The Rule gives us some ancient precedents and principles that work well in modern monasteries and for faithful families in the world. It is a blessing of St. Benedict for all who seek to be children of God.

## Chapter 60

# The Admission of Priests to the Monastery

Monasticism was originally a lay movement. Monks were encouraged to flee clerical ordination as a source of temptation to pride that came with the often-misunderstood power of church leadership. But some were ordained to minister the sacraments to the monastic community. As monks became more numerous and the church needed truly holy priests, she asked that more be ordained. More monks became priests and more priests became monks to minister to the church as well as monastics. The Rule addresses the balance of lay and clerical monasticism.

The Rule prescribes that if a priest asks to be admitted to the monastery he should not be received too quickly. The emphasis is on the request by the priest of the community, not the other way around. If he persists, he is told that he must embrace the full discipline of the Rule. No mention is made of the normal novitiate as with other candidates, but once a monastic he is treated like everyone else.

Yet, the ordained are not disdained either. He may be allowed to stand next to the abbot, who is presumably a layperson, to give the blessing and to celebrate the Mass if the abbot allows. The abbot ordinarily gives the blessing at the Work of God. Otherwise, the priest-monk is to observe the Rule like all the monks and be a special example of humility in light of his clerical call to service. He takes his assigned place in *statio*, normally being seated by rank according to the date of his entry, just like all others. The abbot may choose to give some priests a seat in the middle of rank. The only extra honor he is given is during the Mass. At all other times he is treated like any other lay monk.

As monasteries developed into the Middle Ages they generally became more clerical. Abbots became priests, and since monasteries were already seen as quasi-churches, they were given bishops' powers over monks and laity on monastic lands. Monasteries separated choir monks and lay brothers into two expressions within one community. Choir monks did the clerical work of contemplatives and ministry, while lay brothers did the manual labor of the monastery. Other categories were also developed for *conversi* who did not make formal vows but wore the habit and domestics who did not wear the habit. Only clerics could fill major leadership roles. It worked out very well, but the lay abbot of St. Benedict's time was largely eliminated.

Today clerics and laity are monks of equal status in most monasteries. Both tend to be well educated. In all but the ministry of the sacraments they are equal members of one monastery. Clergy and laity are honored equally and respect is given to each unique role. The church still requires that abbots be priests, unless part of a lay-oriented monastery, but there is a genuine trend to return to the original vision of St. Benedict while conserving the blessings received through centuries of healthy development. At Little Portion we follow the more ancient pattern.

The Rule is a special blessing to us who seek to find the true dignity of both states of life today. Monasteries are schools of God where this gift can be especially practiced and taught to the church in general. It is one of the blessings of St. Benedict.

## Chapter 61

# The Reception of Visiting Monks

Most monks like to visit other monasteries. Regardless of different houses, congregations, and reforms, monks recognize a common calling within one another that unites them all. When traveling on monastery ministry or business, staying in another house is like staying in a home away from home. It is a blessing.

The Rule says that when monks present themselves they are received warmly as monastic family members. The visiting monk is content with the things in the house that might be different from his own. He is at peace with whatever is offered, not making demands that would upset the peace of his hosts. If he can do this he can usually stay as long as necessary. If not, he must move on. If he does find some irregularity or has constructive suggestions, he can present them to the abbot in a humble fashion without pride. It might be that God sent him.

Sometimes monks find they want to stay in the house they visit. If there has been enough time to judge their character, this might be mutually acceptable, but they must receive permission from their home abbot to transfer. If it is given they may proceed. The good of all concerned is the goal.

Once the change has been made, the abbot might place them wherever he chooses in *statio* and rank. They are not entering as novices but come with monastic experience that can bring wisdom. The abbot has the power to make this decision based on the evidence of their life. They might be of great help to the monastery.

Today most monks stay in the house where they professed stability but travel more frequently than ancient monks, so they often stay in other monastic houses. They might also be assigned to make new foundations from that motherhouse. During continuing education or special ministries they might stay as long-term guests in another monastery. Mutual hospitality is the rule, and those who visit practice good monastic manners. It is an acquired art that is mutually beneficial. We eventually learn how to be good guests and good hosts. Occasionally monastics transfer from one house to another but usually for the sake of greater contemplation or solitude. It is not just for personal likes or dislikes. It is for fulfillment in Christ.

At Little Portion we have had good and bad monastic guests. Most of those from other established houses are wonderful and a great blessing to our community. A few inexperienced ones have done some unintended harm. A very few are just troublesome, and we have asked them to leave. Some we do not receive in the first place. But most of these are either gyrovagues who wander from place to place under false pretenses or are in a shaky relationship with their own monastery. They often did not get along well at home so they do not get along very well anywhere. This is always sad.

We live in a time when people travel frequently. Some of these are monks, some associate as oblates with a monastery, and some just have monastic hearts. The Rule helps us to be better travelers and better hosts. It is one of the blessings of Benedict.

## Chapter 62

## The Priests of the Monastery

Monasteries are quasi-churches and microcosms of the church. While originally lay in character and centered on the Divine Office for their daily schedule, they always celebrated the Eucharist on Sundays and feast days. Priests and deacons were present from the earliest days of the Desert Fathers and Mothers. Mentioned in chapter 60, they are also referred to here in the Rule of St. Benedict.

The Rule says the abbot initiates the ordination process for the monks. Natural spiritual leaders are chosen. They do not choose the call. The call chooses them and is largely discerned by the lay community and abbot.

Those chosen for ordination are not to become proud. To ensure this the Rule says that they must be even more obedient to the abbot and the community rule than ever before. They make even greater progress in God now that they are ordained and do not presume that ordination gains them automatic interior closeness to God. It is a fearsome responsibility. What a blessing when this comes together in a man.

They do not hold any special position in the community because of ordination except the sacramental duties of the altar. The ancient monastic caution of ordination is still heard echoing in the words of the Rule. Only the abbot may give him a higher place in *statio* for the genuine good of him and the community.

If equal treatment is offensive to the ordained monk and he refuses to live according to the Rule, he is thought a rebel and not a priest. As with all monastic discipline in the Rule, he is warned a few times. If he fails to amend, the bishop is brought in to help. If even that does not work, he is dismissed from the monastery.

Most modern monasteries are clerical and lay in nature. Ordination was simply part of the process of the educated monk from the Middle Ages until recently. Now it is an option and not an agenda. Clerical pride can still raise its ugly head. But so can anticlericalism. Monasteries are places where such pride is slowly and sometimes not so easily extracted. But the resulting humility is the real glory of both states of life.

At Little Portion we have had a few seek clerical ordination. It has yet to work. Most who put themselves forward have ultimately never seen it or monastic life through to completion. Often pride is still the motivator and other problems remain. But we wait in joyful hope for the day when some of our members will be ordained to minister the sacraments to us. Until then we still rely on chaplains. Most of these are older and wiser priests where the years of experience make them a genuine blessing to the community. But they are older and there are few to replace this most precious treasure from God. We are waiting.

Today the Eucharist is central to sacramental worship. The number of ordained priests is dwindling. Some young ones are servants, and some are still motivated by spiritual pride. Benedict gives us guidelines for discernment that are a blessing.

Chapter 63

# Community Rank

The monastery is a family. A mother or father remains a parent for life. Older siblings always remain the elders. The complexions of these relationships develop as all grow older. Children care for aging parents, and younger siblings even care for elders. But the basic relationship never changes. The Rule addresses this spiritual family in the monastery.

In a monastery this is seen in community rank. Rank is not determined by one's natural age but by the date of entrance into the community. This is a spiritual family, so nature's young will sometimes lead the old, but the abbot and the community can also move a person higher or lower based on their spiritual and communal life. It is dynamic and alive, not static. It is based on Spirit, not law alone.

The younger ones respect their spiritual elders, and elders must love their juniors. The elders address the younger ones as "Brother," and the younger monks address the elders as "Venerable Father." This has nothing to do with the titles of the priest and the laity in the secular church. It is distinctly monastic but has something to teach the secular church as well. The abbot is addressed as "Lord" or "Abbot" out of honor for Christ, not for himself alone.

When they meet, the junior asks for the elder monk's blessing. Juniors always rise up out of respect for the elder, offer their seat, and do not sit again until the elder invites them to do so. Children are always kept in rank and generally are not allowed to associate with the adults until they become professed monks, though they remain under adult supervision. All the monks throughout the monastery may appropriately discipline children.

This has much to teach us in our most casual society today. We have lost a sense of respect and love for one another and the cultural norms that help establish and maintain it. But these norms can be abused by elders or resented by juniors if pride is still present in their practice. The Rule does not support this.

Today most monasteries are more casual but try to maintain the intent of this chapter. Rank is maintained in the church choir stalls, chapter house, and dining room. Abbots and elders are respected by most of the younger monks. The abbot and fathers have a general love for the juniors as spiritual children. Titles are used for the abbots, priors, and priests. Most others just go by brother or sister alone. But a real sense of equality is also maintained for the sake of mutual love and respect.

At Little Portion we are much the same. The inclusion of children makes this of special interest. Children are loved by their extended family, but they show respect for their elders. They do not go first in lines or interrupt. Most of this is what the adults were taught when we were raised, but it is being lost in our culture today. The monastery is a place where it can be reestablished in a healthy and life-giving way. This, in turn, will form our children into better adults who practice mutual respect and love for all. This is a blessing of the Rule of St. Benedict.

# Chapter 64

# The Election of the Abbot

Monastic rules develop from the life of the community and guide us as we develop further. These last chapters of the Rule appear to have been added by Benedict or the later communities as they developed. Even the preceding chapters appear in some order but not in a fully coherent fashion. There are clear interruptions. This indicates that chapters were added as needed for community life.

We are much the same in our spiritual life today. We have basic ideas of our spiritual life at the beginning. They work out pretty well, but we amend, add, and perhaps even drop some as we gain more experience. The Rule inspires and guides us to do this with wisdom and moderation.

The abbot is addressed at the onset of the Rule in chapter 2. This current chapter addresses the election of a new abbot and what to do if you have a really bad one. It also repeats some of the qualities necessary for a good abbot. But it leaves some areas open to interpretation and development. The Rule was still a work in progress.

The entire community, or a part of the community that has sound judgment, elects the abbot. They are elected according to the soundness of their character and not by political conspiracy of lukewarm or evil monks. If they elect a bad abbot who will not direct according to the

Rule, the local bishops and lay Christians can block the conspiracy. Modern election checks and balances are based on this early principle.

The qualities of the abbot are again listed but with some helpful additions. He is to seek not his own preeminence or importance but the welfare of the monastery alone. He is a pastor, not a politician. He is chaste, temperate, and merciful but does not allow abuses. He must hate faults but love the brothers. He avoids extremes in discipline. Too much or too little cause equal harm. He strives to be "loved rather than feared" (64.15), a classic line for leadership in the Rule. He is not an excitable man who agitates the community through his own agitation or litigious religious obsession. Such people are never at rest and never allow others to rest either. He arranges everything in the monastery so that the "strong always have something to yearn for and the weak have nothing to run from" (64.19).

As a founder and spiritual father I have found these words most helpful. It is easy for leaders to get upset about this or that, including the faults of the members, but this usually reflects our own lack of inner peace and our own faults. Once we find some peace within ourselves, we can share it with others. That peace comes only through the dying and rising of Jesus in our personal life, and it usually takes years to find it. There are no shortcuts. Like Christ, we might have to energetically overturn a few moneychangers' tables from time to time, but this cannot be our constant state of mind. We are pastors, not politicians, and servants, not dictators.

Today, monastics try to elect abbots who are good pastors. When one cannot be found in our community, they may be brought in from another. There are established community and church norms for this today that are fair and balanced. The Rule paved the way for that development. It is a blessing of St. Benedict.

## Chapter 65

# The Prior

As a spiritual family, monasteries have both parents and firstborn children. "Prior" means "first," and the prior is the leader immediately under and after the abbot, the spiritual father. Monasteries are also practical places where order is maintained so that the business of community and ministry can be accomplished well. The prior is the abbot's assistant and right-hand person. Ideally, he is a pure spiritual son of the abbot in all things.

The Rule provides for a prior in the monastery, but the Rule only cautiously allows for a prior. The prior had been established by some earlier monastic traditions. It had also become a problem when pride compelled the prior to set up his own little kingdom and even compete with the abbot for authority. Sons can rebel against fathers. Instead of being assistants to their abbots, they thought of themselves as little abbots, used tyrannical leadership styles, and stirred up trouble for the community and the abbot.

The text mentions one of the causes of this problem: bishops appointing both the abbot and the prior. The Rule is clear that the abbot, who is elected by the community and confirmed by the bishop, appoints the prior. When the bishop appoints both, it is an open invitation to envy, rivalry, confusion, and such. The Rule is most critical of this ancient monastic and church leadership problem.

In the monasteries of the Rule the primary leadership role of the abbot is unquestioned. Ordinarily he delegates his authority to the deans mentioned earlier (see chap. 21). Only if he thinks it best in local conditions, and if the community has humbly requested it, does he appoint a prior. The prior is to be the abbot's helper and keep the Rule with greater discipline than all others as an example. If he does not do this, he is warned up to four times. If he still does not change, he is to be deposed. If he persists in resistance after that, he is to be expelled from the monastery. Nevertheless, all discipline is applied with the love and humility of a father.

Little Portion is an integrated monastery. We do not have a formal abbot and prior but a spiritual father and mother who are general and vicar general ministers (either can be general). We also have elders of each expression of the community who form a general council under the general minister. A pro vicar leads when the father and mother are both absent. We also have work heads that report to the council. Vicars only to do what the general approves. The community respects the spiritual father and mother but also the vicars and elders who have their delegated authority.

We tend to rotate secondary leadership positions among various qualified members so that more get to know the greater burden of leadership. This makes us all better members, but we have found that some misuse it. Often the ones who want greater community input are most feared by others when they become leaders. This betrays a need for control. Sometimes the burden of long-term leadership is too much for a member. The Rule teaches us to share leadership responsibly and not to abuse it. Once learned, it becomes a blessing from Benedict that works for leaders anywhere.

## Chapter 66

## The Porter of the Monastery

Monasteries are in the world but not of it. They are separated from all but united with all. The original monasteries in Egypt were scattered hermit's cells within a day's walk of a common center and church. Pachomius, Shenoute, and others monasticized entire small villages with a cenobium. Some of these were walled fortresses to protect against marauders. In the West monasteries ranged from houses and villas of wealthy converts to urban centers attached to churches to rural, self-enclosed complexes for prayer, ministry, and all that was necessary for monastic life. Benedict's monasteries were of the latter kind.

The porter is the gatekeeper of the monastery. He is stationed at the main entrance and greets all who come to the door. He stops unwanted guests. He takes messages and gives replies back and forth between visitors and monks. He is sensible enough to act as a kind of monastic receptionist. He is older so he will not be tempted to run around outside the monastery.

He has a room at the door of the monastery so he can quickly greet those who seek entrance. His greeting is never worldly or secular but clearly religious in nature. He speaks gently but clearly about God in his responses.

He is not a mere receptionist but a monastic porter. Like other monastic workers, he is given a younger assistant if necessary.

The Rule then mentions monastic enclosure. This means more than mere privacy here. The monastery is to be constructed so that everything necessary for monastic life is found within and there is little need for monks to roam around outside the monastery. It is a substantially self-supportive and self-enclosed unit. This is so important that Benedict wants this chapter read often to the brothers so they can give no excuse of ignorance. This is significant.

We live in a very mobile culture. People are on the go daily. We are unstable and rarely really at home. Monasteries also suffer from this. Some monks are always on the lookout for a way to go out for this or that. This always betrays a deeper instability that a trip to town will not cure. The real solution is hunkering down in monastic solitude and community, facing our inner demons, and bringing them to the cross and resurrection of Jesus. The enclosure helps us find this blessing.

Today, monasteries are interdependent with others, but we must also be self-supportive. We are ready to work with the culture but must also be ready to be countercultural. Our monastic enclosure helps ready us even if the electricity or the energy for transporting foodstuffs and such is cut off. We can make a few adjustments and carry on. Even as in the Dark Ages, we shine the light of Christ that keeps civilization alive. We have done it before and can do so again.

Porters ensure that the enclosure for the outer and inner peace of the monastic spiritual family is protected and maintained. It is a blessing of St. Benedict.

## Chapter 67

# Brothers Sent on a Journey

The enclosure of the previous chapter insulates the community from the harsh environment of the world but it cannot isolate it. Jesus does not want us to be worldly, but he still sends us into the world to save it. In the process, we find salvation for ourselves. Monasteries have normal daily ministry and business interactions with the secular and ecclesial world. It is a simple fact of life.

Earlier chapters mentioned the clothing of traveling monastics and eating outside the monastery (see chaps. 50–51). This chapter addresses whether or not we become worldly by venturing into the world. We deal with material reality without becoming materialistic, and produce things for consumption without becoming consumeristic. The Rule presents some procedures that help us with this weakness found among even monastics.

Those going on a journey first ask for the prayers of the abbot and community before leaving. The community prays for them while they are absent. When they return, they lie facedown before all and ask forgiveness for any faults during the journey. This sacramentalizes the journey and makes it a journey with Jesus.

Those who return from the world are not to spread worldly news and gossip. This upsets the peace of the monastery. Those who do are to be corrected, as are any who presume to leave on their own without the knowledge and approval of the abbot and the community.

At Little Portion we must travel outside as well. We operate a large monastic household, ministries, and farm. This becomes very complicated and unwieldy if not coordinated. We try to coordinate trips with the needs of others and keep them to a minimum. This is just good economics. We also communicate with the leaders and community members individually and in chapter when we must go out. This helps everyone coordinate and is common courtesy in a family.

We are careful not to spread any gossip we hear outside. The news may be true, but it might not be good to share it with everyone or in public. Yet we pray for real needs of friends and neighbors. We keep up with the local, national, and global news through periodicals and the internet but do not watch cable or network TV. There is a healthy balance in this that can be maintained through intentional discipline.

We do not use the sacramental prayers mentioned in the Rule except for special trips and ministries. Medical trips and major ministries and business meetings are most important and are prayed for. The daily stuff is coordinated with the council and the weekly chapter, and general permissions suffice for ongoing traveling needs. There is a real sense that when one travels, everyone goes with them and supports them in their journey. We are never alone. Jesus and the community are always with us. This is a great blessing from the ancient Rule of St. Benedict.

Chapter 68

## The Assignment of Impossible Tasks to a Brother

Monastics highly value listening and functional obedience or we would not even join a monastery. We sincerely want to do what is asked of us. We believe we hear God in it. But what do we do when we are asked something that simply seems impossible for us to do? It is a question we all face sooner or later. The answer determines whether or not we can live as monastics in a community.

This has been quickly addressed in chapters 5 and 7. It is mentioned again here as a rather obvious insertion to emphasize and develop the point after further experience. But it does not change the initial teaching found earlier.

This does not seem to include the case where we are assigned something that is physically impossible through illness, injury, or defect, though it is not excluded. It seems to be more a matter of one's general constitution, abilities, and skills.

The first response of the monk is to accept the obedience with gentleness, not with immediate reaction or resistance. If the task turns out to be impossible to fulfill, we go to the superior and quietly explain our reasons why we think the task might be best suited for another. But we do this without pride, obstinacy, or refusal to do the task. If the superior still asks us to do it, we ask for God's help and genuinely do the best we can without hesitation. This is a tall order, but it can be done with God's help. God never calls us to something he does not give us the grace to fulfill.

Today, we add the situation where we are asked to do something against our conscience. If asked to do something against the teaching of the church in matters of faith or morality, or the rule and constitutions of our community, we cannot obey. Nevertheless, we do not reject the authority of the leader either. Only if this becomes serious and habitual may we take more action to correct an abuse of power. It may or may not be intentional. If abusive, the community and the church give us procedures for these occasions that protect both the community and the individual.

Most problems with obedience have more to do with little things that bring to light bigger matters of personal preference and pride. Sometimes we have been asked to do something we do not like or want to do. But that is precisely where obedience is tested and strengthened. It is an opportunity for growth.

At Little Portion we organically grow most of our own food. We joke that we must all learn how to "grow a green bean for God." Sometimes we are asked to grow them differently than we did when we were raised on our "daddy and mama's farm." Sometimes we just do not want to work outside in the hot or cold. We may not like or agree with it fully, but there is nothing immoral or against the community rule in what we are being asked to do. In that case we simply learn how to do it. We quietly and joyfully obey. We do not grumble and complain to others or ourselves. Then we are truly free. This is a key for learning inner listening and freedom in every outer situation. It is a blessing of St. Benedict.

## Chapter 69

# The Presumption of Defending Another in the Monastery

Jesus wants us to defend the poor and oppressed. It is a theme of the Gospel. But in monasteries this can often be misguided and downright destructive. The Rule of Benedict addresses this dynamic in cenobitical monasteries.

He says that we are not to "presume" to defend another in the monastery. Presumption is the issue. There are often other forces of healing correction at work during communal discipline that we are not all privy to. These fall under the jurisdiction of the abbot or his delegates. Sometimes we can short-circuit these healing measures if we intervene without full knowledge of the situation. We think we are doing well, but we may be doing harm instead.

He also mentions the presence of blood relatives in monasteries that can complicate the process. This was not uncommon in earlier times. Entire families joined monasteries, and blood relatives often found themselves within a larger spiritual family under an abbot or abbess. It could be tough to see a brother or sister, son or daughter, father or mother disciplined in community. It would be unnatural if there were no loyalty there. Families are a gift of God. But we give up more limited earthly families to become a part of a bigger spiritual one in a monastery. This dynamic also happens with spiritual friends in monasteries. The notion of spiritual friendship is old, valued, and venerable. But so is the caution against exclusive friendships that form bonds that preclude obedience in the broader monastic family. Our friendships are inclusive and healing, not exclusive and divisive.

But there is a time to defend a brother when they are wronged through community politics and intrigue. This is done in appropriate private and community meetings, not through gossip. We do well to remember the Desert Father who cautioned monks about judging another, for we all have sins that have not been brought to light yet. Charity and not punishment are always the motivation for any disciplinary action.

Today most discipline in a monastery comes after much patience and input from a number of folks. It is never an arbitrary action or administered lightly. It is usually done in private so as not to embarrass. Sometimes it is brought before various configurations of community so that everyone may speak. But we try not to gang up on a person at fault. Confidential details are never broken intentionally but held sacred. Words are spoken honestly but in love. The tone is healing, not punitive.

At Little Portion we have seen well-meaning folks defend others when they do not know all the history or facts of a situation. What is needed is a united and consistent communal voice calling the member to healing through loving discipline. This takes trust, and we are not always good at trust. When others intrude into that process they assume that they know more than the superiors or community who have been pastorally addressing a member for some time. It rarely works. The Rule reminds us to do all things coordinated together in a loving and truthful way for the genuine healing of another. It is a blessing of St. Benedict.

## Chapter 70

## The Presumption of Striking Another Monk at Will

Jesus was a man of peace. He did not strike but was struck. He offered no resistance, even when he was resisted. He took the blows we deserve, healing those who offered and received them through love. He also showed his authority by living under God's authority. Monastics try to be universally like Christ. The Rule helps us by addressing the presumptive use of force and violence within a monastery.

The Rule addresses the presumption of striking another without the approval of the abbot or seniors. Interestingly, the primary problem was presumption and not correction, pride and not punishment, violence and not force. Only the abbot could delegate specific communal correction. Any adult monastic with the abbot's general approval corrected children. Force, not violence, was used as a last measure. It was administered in communal humility, not self-will and pride.

In those days it was acceptable to use force as a final attempt to bring an errant person back to the right way after all else failed. This shocks modern sensibility, but they used every available means at their disposal to help another person to change for the better. Corporal correction was an accepted means at that time. Monks used force, but when rightly administered it was not considered violence.

The Rule warns against violence. There is a classical difference between force and violence. Force is controlled and is done for the good of another. Violence is done out of anger and does little or no good for anyone. The problem with corporal correction is that the line between force and violence is sometimes very thin. It is best to minimize its use or avoid it altogether. We are all still sinners. But discipline is still needed.

Corporal correction is not used with adults in monasteries today. Other means have proven more helpful and effective. Parents may use it sparingly with their children. We are watchful for abuse. We have rarely seen any violence with adults at Little Portion. I have only seen one fight between brothers in over thirty years. Those prone to violence cannot live in a monastery. They either change or leave.

The entire Rule is an attempt to remove violence from the soul in Christ through monastic obedience to a rule and abbot in community. Monasticism is a way of peace, not of violence.

There is also a violence of words and attitudes. This still happens in monasteries. I have seen it at Little Portion. Sometimes we speak down to others to build ourselves up in God's name, not to build others up in God. Sometimes attitudes are dismissive, confrontational, and coarse, not gentle, peaceful, and kind. These can be as hurtful as blows and sometimes cause even greater emotional harm to sensitive souls. It is shameful for monastics. Monks are called to be at peace within and instruments of peace for others. The Rule addresses presumption and violence. Albeit from a different culture, place, and time, it is a timeless blessing of St. Benedict.

## Chapter 71
# Mutual Obedience

Monks are obedient to the abbot for the sake of obedience to Christ. And we are obedient to the abbot to teach us how to be obedient to all the brothers and sisters. It is practice for mutual obedience. Obedience means listening deeply and respectfully and letting go of our own opinions when expressions of ego and self-will surface. This chapter is about mutual obedience between everyone in the monastery.

Mutual obedience is first expressed to elder monks who are not necessarily in formal positions of authority. Elder members have more experience. Juniors show them respect and love for the wisdom learned through experience and care for them as they grow older in years. If a monk is reproved by the abbot or seniors and senses that an elder is also disturbed with their fault, they immediately go to ask forgiveness of them as well. They do this profoundly by prostrating at their feet. Anyone not willing to do this is seriously disciplined. Those who cannot change are asked to leave the monastery. Mutual obedience is of primary importance. Without it monasteries become truly terrible places to live.

Today monasteries are usually places where elders are valued as precious treasures of experience. They are loved and respected, even though they are not in formal leadership. They are spiritual fathers and mothers and elder brothers and sisters. When this is present in a monastery it becomes a special place of love and respect that flows out to all.

New members are a gift of the Spirit to communities, and Benedict values their input at proper places and times. Nevertheless, younger members sometimes think they know all the answers and even make fun of or resent older monks. Hopefully, this youthful arrogance under the appearance of zeal wears off pretty quickly. They make their own fair share of mistakes and learn to listen. Then they can stay. If they persevere they also come round to wisdom. Eventually we are all elders.

At Little Portion we have kind of grown into this gift. At first most of us were young in monastic life. Only our spiritual mother came after twenty-five years in another community. We all had our own opinions about monastic life. We disagreed a lot. Sometimes we even argued. Many left but some stayed. Those who stayed eventually grew into this marvelous monastic gift of mutual obedience. There is no way to learn it but with patience and time. We Americans are not always good with this. We are often impatient and want things right now. The Rule teaches us a different way.

Mutual obedience and listening are marvelous gifts in monasteries. These gifts make them special places where heaven comes to earth. It starts with the abbot and delegated leaders and branches out to everyone. The way we treat our elders is especially telling of how we treat everyone. We Americans are not always good with obedience. For us, it is all about function. Even then we are often suspicious of it. But mutual obedience is a deeper mystical charism that changes everything in our life. It turns the bitter to sweet in Christ. It is one of the greatest gifts of St. Benedict.

Chapter 72

# The Good Zeal of Monks

"Prefer nothing whatever to Christ" (72.11). This is one of the strongest and often-repeated quotes from the Rule. It is found at the end but is implied throughout. Jesus is the Alpha and Omega, the beginning and the end of our faith as Christians. It is especially true for Christian monks.

But the monastic understanding of Jesus is far more than mere correct doctrine about Catholic or ecumenical Christian faith and morality, church and monastery structures, or the correct performance of liturgy and sacraments. It is a life experience. We become "like Christ," or "Christian." Perhaps that is why monastics have always been both protectors of orthodoxy and pioneers in ecumenical and interfaith dialogue. They have also been great missionaries to bring the real Jesus to people who are hungry for something more than just another religious institution.

Monks are zealous but not zealots, radical but not fanatical, and built squarely on founding fundamentals without becoming fundamentalists. We strive not to become lukewarm or take our faith for granted. We try to be appropriately zealous in our love of God and one another. We not only pray but also become a prayer.

The monastery of Benedict is cenobitical, or, more strictly, communal. This good zeal is a daily experience that is tested in rather close quarters with others who are trying to do the same thing, but it is not automatic. We must take the initiative in showing respect, being patient with each other's weaknesses, and acting in obedience to leaders and members. Like communal prayer, it is a work of God.

Mostly we live not for ourselves but for God and one another. We relinquish our self-will and private opinions in favor of a greater will of God found through community. In this we rediscover our original human will in God and are more fulfilled as people than ever before through the divine gift in Jesus. This is found not in some esoteric ideology or place but right here in the ordinary things of daily life with others in a monastery. It is a divine call that is found with one's feet planted firmly on the ground.

Today it is reported that Christianity is becoming one of the most persecuted religions on earth. This is growing right here in the West. Perhaps we have brought some of this on ourselves by not really living the faith we profess. When the world looks to Christians sometimes they do not see Christ. This jeopardizes the integrity of our witness for Christ.

The Rule of St. Benedict challenges that defect. It clearly calls us back to a life in Jesus Christ that is authentic and real. It is both mystical and practical. It is loving and true. It is learned and tested in the monastery that is a "school of the Lord's service," and it is shared with all who visit. It makes a monastery of every home and every monastery a true spiritual home. It makes the community a real family and every family a domestic church in Christ. It is one of the blessings of St. Benedict.

Chapter 73

# The Rule: Only a Beginning of Perfection

The Rule ends with a statement of humility. Benedict calls it only "a little rule for beginners." But it has become the most widespread monastic rule in the Christian West. Great things always have small beginnings, and great works begin with humble attitudes of service. That is how it was with the Rule of St. Benedict.

The last few chapters of the Rule take us back to the beginning source of the Rule itself: Jesus and obedience. They form a kind of summary and great amen to the broader text of the Rule. One of those amens is the greater monastic tradition that transcends East or West. It is a monasticism that is truly universal.

The Rule builds on and integrates the various monastic traditions that came before it. Perhaps that is why it could climb so high? Yet, it says it is only a beginning. Those interested in deeper roots are referred back to the early sources of the great monastic founders before Benedict. The specific sources mentioned are Scripture; the Catholic fathers; the monastic fathers; the *Institutes* and *Conferences*, presumably of John Cassian; and the rules of St. Basil, the father of Eastern monasticism. They are themselves a summary of a tradition that preceded them.

This tradition is rich and multilayered. It is simple but is far from simplistic. The more we discover, the more questions arise and the more we study. Study leads to prayer, and prayer leads to life. Instead of being discouraged, we are encouraged to live a developing monasticism today in our own culture and environment. We are part of a living tradition that is rich and full. Jesus came to bring us life abundantly, and monastic life is no exception.

An interesting dimension here is the integration of the original hermit and communal monastic ways. In chapter 1 the Rule says that the fewer numbered hermits live a superior monastic way of life. Yet he also says that the cenobium is the better way for most. Monastic history began with hermits and developed from loose colonies to formal communities. Yet monasticism has always included the way of the hermit as an option for the few who seek it. This can be partial or total. This has taken various expressions through history and is possible in most monasteries today. But it is only for those who have first been tested in community life for many years. The cenobium provides the sure foundation even for the Christian hermit.

The monastery is the environment from which to climb to the summit of spiritual life in Christ, but it is up to each of us to make the climb. The monastery is only the outer aid for the monk within us all and the cell for the hermit within. It is the cave of the heart that is most important. Without reaching the interior home, the external tools of the house are in vain. The soul is the hermit within, and our bodies are our cells we take into the cloister of the entire world. Once we learn to live in the monastery well, the entire world becomes a monastery for us. If we have made the monastery our home, we are everywhere at home and make a monastery of every home. This is perhaps the greatest blessing of all from St. Benedict. God bless you!